RUNNING
THE LYDIARD WAY
by Arthur Lydiard with Garth Gilmour

World Publications, Inc.
P.O. Box 366 Mountain View, CA 94042

Recommended Reading:
Runner's World Magazine, $9.50/year
Write Box 366, Mt. View, CA 94042
for a free catalog of publications and supplies
for runners and other athletes.

Originally published 1978 by
Hodder & Stoughton, Auckland, London, Sydney.

Library of Congress Number 78-360
ISBN 0-89037-096-6

Contents

Photographs

Part I Training and Racing

The 1977 "Round the Bays" run is an 11.27-kilometer race in Auckland, New Zealand. With 20,000 competitors, it is the largest race in the world. (Photograph courtesy of the Auckland Joggers Club.)

Part II Preparation and Fitness

Athletes warming up before competition. (Photograph by Paul J. Sutton.)

Part III Special Training

Six- and seven-year-olds on the run. (Photograph by David H. Zinman.)

Part IV International Coaching

Arthur Lydiard explaining training techniques. (Photograph by Dave Drennan.)

Appendix Training Schedules

Runners crossing the Verrazano-Narrows Bridge in the 1977 New York City Marathon. Some of the top finishers are (left to right): Ron Hill (2), Jerome Drayton (4), Brian Maxwell (behind Drayton), Carl Hatfield (27), Tom Fleming (10), Ian Thompson (1), and winner Bill Rodgers (3). (Photograph by Richard Benyo.)

Foreword

In 1961, in the foreword to the first edition of *Run to the Top,* this book's predecessor, I wrote: "Arthur Lydiard is one of the outstanding athletic coaches of all time." Now, sixteen years later, I am obliged to correct that. It is doubtful anyone will ever have the impact Lydiard has had on the approach to physical conditioning as a prerequisite to sporting efforts.

Arthur Lydiard was relatively unknown in 1961. Few understood the athletic revolution he had begun, not many expected him to repeat his initial world-class successes, and there was even the impression abroad that he exerted some mystic influence to achieve results. Lydiard was certainly capable of inspiring his runners. But now the whole world knows of the Lydiard system of training, conditioning, and development that brought about those successes. Most of the world's coaches and athletes employ it, or close imitations of it.

Lydiard has made his methods freely available to anyone who wants to use them. His system has been applied to conditioning rugby players, cyclists, canoeists, squash players, and gridiron men. It has a place in every sport, because its fundamental aim is a high level of fitness on which to build the specific skills a sportsman needs.

The system has caused a worldwide interest, and belief, in the benefits of jogging for all age groups. East Germany has even based a complete national fitness program on Lydiard's concepts of jogging and fitness. The results of this program were evident at the Montreal Olympics, when East Germany demonstrated the most dramatic sporting advances since Lydiard's runners began middle- and long-distance track domination in the early sixties.

Since 1961, the Lydiard system has been streamlined to a degree, but it is still basically the same one that fired Peter Snell, Murray Halberg, and Barry Magee to their initial eminence in Rome in 1960—and swept Lydiard to fame with them.

Lydiard didn't evolve the system from a desire to produce champions, to change the running world, or even to become a champion himself. In 1945, he played football, and was an occasional athlete using haphazard and casual training methods. He suddenly realized he was not as fit as he'd thought. He worried about the shape he would be in ten or twenty years, and began experimenting. The experiment, which lasted more than a decade, was initially conducted on himself, but gradually attracted the interest of younger runners.

To test himself practically, he returned to active athletics. At an age when others in those times would have considered themselves too old, he became a scratch runner over 1 to 3 miles, a provincial cross-country representative, and a contender for national titles. The early competitions revealed serious flaws in his method of attaining fitness, so he continued changing patterns, and gradually evolved his basic theory: *that long, even-paced running at a strong speed increases strength and endurance, even when it is continued. close to the point of collapse; it is beneficial, not harmful, to regular competition.* A need to perfect his system drove him to further refinements.

Lydiard was now battering himself over mountain-country runs up to 50 kilometers, determined to find the limit of human endurance and, along with it, the formula for successful competitive running. He was growing older, but also fitter, so he turned to the marathon. He soon found that by training for marathons he could run even faster on the track than he'd run before. The key was in his hand.

Then one of his early pupils, after two years of trailing Lydiard on his lonely runs, whipped a provincial championship field by 80 meters—a gap he established in the first lap and held until the end. That run established Lydiard as a coach, a qualification he neither sought nor particularly wanted. The lad, Lawrie King, went on to be New Zealand cross-country champion, 6-mile record-holder, and 1954 Empire and Commonwealth Games representative.

By this time, Lydiard was New Zealand's top marathon runner, bringing a sophistication and challenge to a race that had long been regarded as the occupation of mental deficients. He ran for New Zealand in the 1960 Empire and Commonwealth Games, during the period when he was still struggling to find his peaks at the right time. There he ran what he called a "poor 13th."

He retired from competitive running in 1967 to concentrate on making enough money to establish himself in business, but by then he had a school of pupils, including Halberg and Magee. Lydiard knew his runners. He'd worked with Halberg only a year when, in 1953, he predicted that in several years Halberg would be the greatest middle-distance runner New Zealand had known—Lovelock included—and would begin toppling world records. Seven years later, Halberg took the 5,000 meters in Rome, became a sub-four-minute miler, and went on to a string of world records. Snell carried through another bold early prediction, when he became the half-mile and mile sensation of the 1960s. He is still probably the most brilliant runner the world has seen, John Walker and Filbert Bayi included.

By the mid-1950s, Lydiard had virtually completed his promise. He knew how and when to mix the ingredients—the long marathon-type mileages, the hill work, the leg-speed work, the sprint training, the sharpening and freshening—and how to time the mixture to send his runners to the starting line at their exact peaks. As the sporting world began to stir with interest, he and his team ignored everyone else and helped themselves generously to all the New Zealand middle- and long-distance titles. In nine seasons from 1954, they won 45 of the 63 gold medals presented for the half-mile, mile, 3 miles, 6 miles, marathon, steeplechase, and cross-country, including all the miles and all the sixes. Minor placings, too, became even more numerous as the Lydiard school grew and prospered.

Then came Rome. Lydiard then knew all the answers, although he didn't yet know how to achieve them. He had only the most basic knowledge of physiology and the mechanics of the human body. But he knew his system worked because he'd spent more than a decade making it work.

Since 1960, however, his knowledge has become vast. He can now sit with physiologists and sports medicine experts and not only speak their language, but also suggest new concepts. He can inspire coaches and athletes of all nations to get out and follow him, although there will always be those who dispute his techniques and his theories. Yet even among the critics, there are many who secretly practice exactly what Lydiard preaches (with minor variations to convince themselves that they thought of it first).

Lydiard's target in 1945 was to make himself fit to enjoy life in 1965. He overshot his target—and the whole world has enjoyed the rewards in human endeavor, triumph over the stopwatch, and newfound belief in the acquisition and preservation of glowing health.

The greatest coach? I don't make the claim lightly—or alone. Bill Bowerman, in his book *Coaching Track and Field,* wrote: "There is no better distance coach in the world."

For this first time since 1961, here is everything Arthur Lydiard knows.

Garth Gilmour
Auckland/New Plymouth
New Zealand
1977

Introduction

My recent years have been a great deal different from my beginnings as a coach in the early 1950s. When I first coached in New Zealand and had around me in my Auckland suburb of Owairaka all those good athletes the world later came to know—Murray Halberg, Peter Snell, Jeff Julian, Bill Baillie, Ray Puckett, Barry Magee, and others—there were few problems. We minded our own business and went about things in our own way. There were no real pressures and we were able to avoid petty jealousies and snubbing from officials, although I guess at times we must have seemed a pretty arrogant bunch. But once I got those athletes through to Rome and Tokyo, people decided I must know easy and magical ways to train. More and more people became interested in what I was doing, and the whole position changed.

Since I enjoyed helping anyone who was interested, not just those who might be worth training as potential champions, I was inundated with telephone calls and letters. My phone at the shoe factory I was then managing was constantly ringing, and it wasn't to order shoes. I couldn't work properly and it was all suddenly very difficult.

I couldn't say to one athlete, "I'll train you," and to the next, "You, I won't train," just because the first had greater prospects. It became a question of training them all or not training any, and, for me, it was a frustrating position to be in. Offers were coming in from overseas as well—the Finns first approached me as far back as 1961—but I turned these down, mainly because I had a young family and travel was out of the question. Eventually, I was forced to give up my shoe factory position and take on a milk round at night just to be away from people. In short, I had coached myself out of coaching in New Zealand. I was pushed into a situation in which my family, my work, and the involvement of amateur coaching clashed head-on.

Subsequently, I joined Rothmans, New Zealand, as a member of their Sports Foundation. This was a great help to me, since it involved lecturing all around the country.

A further overseas offer, from the Mexicans, inviting me to take a three-year contract from 1966 to the 1968 Olympics in Mexico City, was the final temptation.

By now I was feeling that I wasn't really coaching athletes in New Zealand. Many coaches in New Zealand were not prepared to accept my training methods, and you can't get anywhere without their cooperation. Even if I'd coached three gold medal winners in each of the Olympics since 1960, there would still be people questioning my methods. I became tired of this, and it helped me to make the decision to go to Mexico.

But Mexico was more disillusionment. The athletes were fantastically talented—there is no question of this—but the people in control weren't doing their job properly. They were playing politics. I tried to stick it out, but couldn't. I returned to New Zealand long before the end of my contract period.

I hadn't been home long before the Finns renewed their offer and I accepted it. They were the opposite of the Mexicans. Their officials were realistic, determined to succeed, and backed me all the way. The president and secretary of the Finnish Athletic Federation, Yuka Unilla and Arnis Valsti, respectively, stood solidly behind me so it was just a matter of working along planned lines and ignoring the critics. Time was against me as far as the 1968 Olympics were concerned, but I worked hard in Finland and laid the groundwork. I was there two years, and on the move more or less continually, day and night. I later swore that I would never again do as much for anyone as I did for Finland in those two years. It was too tiring.

From Finland, I went to West Germany to lecture for six weeks, and was asked to set up a program. I also wrote a booklet that they and the Swedes have used extensively since.

The West German physiologists wanted to know what I had discovered in practice so that they could measure it against their scientific theories. The East Germans did exactly the same thing.

They scientifically analyzed what I was doing, developed it as a national program, and, in the process, considerably enlarged my understanding of physiology.

I also lectured in Denmark, and developed a happy relationship with the Danish Athletic Federation and coaches there.

From Europe, I went to Australia for a vacation. It was a wise move. I was mentally and physically jaded, and my own running program had been so disrupted that I was feeling serious ill-effects.

When the Australians learned that I was there, I was invited to accompany Ken Stewart, Australia's Olympic coach in Munich, and two government officials on a trip to assess the athletic potential of the Australian aborigines. This took us to many areas of the far north—Mannengrida and Groote Island around Darwin, the Daly River area, and Uindamor in Central Australia—where the aborigines were being assisted to adjust to the European way of life, particularly now that these areas were being exploited for their mineral resources. I had an interesting two months. We found the aborigines athletically talented but, unfortunately, because of their poor diet, most of them lost their natural endurance after they reached puberty, and didn't develop as they could have. Their ability to jump and play such games as basketball was remarkable. I have no doubt that if they were brought up from childhood on a balanced protein diet, they would become great athletes over a range of sports.

At Uindamor, 320 kilometers northwest of Alice Springs, the local schoolteachers decided to establish a running track. They did this very simply. The got out the station wagon, punched a hole in the bottom of a big tin of french chalk, and then drove in a loop of about 400 meters, letting the chalk trickle out onto the red dust. It was an instant running track. The kids loved the competition.

From Australia, I was invited to the United States for a three-month lecture tour, which eventually lasted eight months. I visited twenty-six states, and, as in Germany, found everyone eager to talk athletics with me. I felt again that I was doing the right kind of job. The American coaches and people are, as they say of themselves, real track nuts. They genuinely love the sport, work hard, and as a result are very successful. The coaches are outstanding—competitive, but also completely cooperative. Various schools may compete with each other, but if people can help each other they certainly do. It's one reason why their sport generally continues to evolve to higher standards. The pooling of knowledge is vital.

While I was in the States, I was invited to Venezuela. I'd vowed never to go to another Latin American country after the Mexican experience. But I was assured Venezuela would be different, and I wouldn't have the problem of dealing with people incapable of doing their jobs or not honest enough to do them straightforwardly. So I went for eight months. I was impressed by Venezuela's athletes, potentially the greatest I have seen. They had great speed, endurance, and dedication. However, it rapidly dawned on me that I was again faced with administrators concerned with playing politics to the detriment of the athletic potential of the country. Once again, I couldn't get straight answers.

I felt very sorry for Dr. Felice Castillo, the president of the athletic federation. He was plainly being hoodwinked by underlings he trusted, and there was nothing I could do about it. At the end of the eight months, I felt I had done all I could hope to do in that difficult situation.

In late 1971, I went back to Denmark for three months on the understanding that I would return for another three months just before Munich. The Danes were cordial and easy to get along with, but they seemed soft and lazy when it came to training. They weren't dour, stubborn, hard people like the Finns; they needed more motivation. They were still on the interval training system, which we'd thrown away years before, and they did nothing in the winter. Admittedly, it is difficult at that time of year. Although the snow and ice melt during the daytime, in the early mornings it's like running on glass. We could hardly stand up, unlike in Finland, where the ice stays dry and the snow firm, since the temperatures are much lower.

While in Munich for the 1972 Games, the Venezuelans asked me to return and help them again. I was approached by Dr. Castillo, and in the end I agreed and went back for about three months. I was still hoping something would rub off on to them but, again, I didn't get very far. The administration they had made it useless. Venezuela could have some of the greatest sprinters and middle- and long-distance runners in the world if they had the right people training them.

Back in New Zealand, I was approached by a large producer

of building materials, Winstone Ltd., and invited to join their public relations staff. This was on the understanding that I would have time to devote to coaching and to act as national middle- and long-distance coach for the New Zealand Amateur Athletic Association. Although I knew there was little possibility of ever coaching athletes again in New Zealand the way I did before, I accepted because I hoped to help the coaches.

In Tokyo in 1964, seven of the athletes on the New Zealand team—five men and two women—were runners I had personally trained. This had pointed up a serious imbalance in athletics in New Zealand. These good athletes had come from in and around Auckland, where I was training, but what of the rest of the country?

But this time around, I was pleasantly surprised to find that the coaches were now prepared to accept the fundamentals of my kind of training. Although they were approaching it in different ways, the basis of their programs was correct. There were now groups of fine athletes developing in various areas of both islands. It was gratifying to note in Montreal that the middle- and long-distance runners on the New Zealand team all had different coaches. It meant I had succeeded in what I had tried to do initially: to give every athlete in New Zealand the chance to train along the lines I had already proved were successful. This augurs well for the future of middle- and long-distance running in New Zealand. The Finns went to the top because their coaches coordinated their training. New Zealand and other countries are now developing the same way.

Wherever I have been, I have also developed and helped organize jogging programs. New Zealand had the first organized jogging group in the world—in Auckland in 1961—but now many other countries have followed. Every village and town in Finland these days has jogging trails. There are many Danes now running for their health, with annual competitions that draw up to thirteen thousand participants. This all has the valuable side effect of motivating more young people to turn to running. This is not merely as a sport, but for health and as a basis of preparation and conditioning for other sports. Nothing pleases me more than to see parents and their children running together. I know it's going to lead to a better way of life and help alleviate cardiac problems, which are killing more and more people.

Part I

Training and Racing

Chapter 1

The Physiology of Exercise

It is impossible to be explicit about the physiological reactions of hard training. But I offer the following reasons for my training approach, based on thirty-five years experience as an athlete and coach and several years of lay study of physiology in conjunction with physiologists and sports medicine institutes.*

I have tried to simplify the theory into practical terms, because it is important to know why exhausting exercise affects you, and how it can be used to maximize athletic efficiency.

Fundamentally, my training system is based on a balanced combination of *aerobic* and *anaerobic* running. Aerobic running means running within your capacity to use oxygen. Each person according to his physical condition, is able to use a certain amount of oxygen each minute. But this limit can be increased by proper exercise.

ANAEROBIC EXERCISE

The aerobic limit, known as the maximum steady state, is the level at which you are working to the limit of your ability to breathe in, transport, and utilize oxygen. When you exercise beyond that maximum steady state, you begin running in an anaerobic state. This is made possible by chemical changes in your body's metabolism. This supplies the oxygen you need over and

*For coaches and athletes who want to explore the subject more deeply than we intend to go in this book, I recommend *The Physiology of Exercise* by Laurence Morehouse and Augustus Miller, a good book based on scientific experience. In most areas, I have found it corresponds with my own practical experience.

above the amount you can breathe in, transport, and utilize. This is a reconversion process with strict limits, so the body is always limited in its anaerobic capacity. The reaction that takes place creates an *oxygen debt,* which can be incurred quickly. Oxygen debt is the amount of oxygen required to counteract anaerobic exercise over and above the oxygen you can gain through your lungs. This is accompanied by the accumulation of lactic acid and other waste products leading directly to neuromuscular breakdown or, simply, tired muscles that refuse to function as you wish. The absolute limit when you are exercising anaerobically is an oxygen debt of approximately 15 liters, although the average athlete will have a limit considerably less than this until he has trained properly.

As exercise increases in intensity, the oxygen debt doubles, squares, and cubes. Experiments by Morehouse and Miller graphically show how dramatically the oxygen requirement increases as the speed of running is raised:

Yards per second	Liters per minute
5.56 to 6.45 An increase of 0.89 yards per second	5.08 to 8.75 An increase in oxygen requirement of 3.67
9.10 to 9.23 An increase of 0.13 yards per second	28.46 to 33.96 An increase in oxygen requirement of 5.50
This shows that when speeds are faster, slight increases in speed demand increasingly larger amounts of oxygen.	

METABOLISM

Metabolism refers to the chemical reactions in living cells by which energy is provided for vital processes. It often refers to the oxidations that are the ultimate source of energy. A muscle converts chemical energy into mechanical activity. It is stimulated by nervous impulses produced through chemical changes. The heart is a muscle. This nervous energy is thought to derive from the breakdown of high-energy compounds, such as adenosine triphosphate (ATP), which results from the oxidation of food stuffs.

Exercise requires continual adjustments in respiration, circulation, temperature-regulating mechanisms, and kidney functions. In fact, the entire body is affected by the metabolic activity that provides energy for exercise.

LACTIC ACID

The energy yields vary widely between aerobic and anaerobic exercise. Morehouse and Miller have shown that aerobic exercise is nineteen times more economical than anaerobic exercise. The more intense the exercise, the quicker and less economically the body's fuel is used, and the faster the waste products accumulate in the form of *lactic acid.* This accumulation increases cell activity, interfering with the activities of *enzymes.* These organic catalysts produced by living cells speed the rate of chemical reactions in the body and assist in the recovery from exhausting work.

Lactic acid also upsets the *blood pH,* the measure of the blood's degree of alkalinity or acidity. The point of neutrality between alkalinity and acidity is 7.0, and normal blood pH is between 7.46 and 7.48, indicating that it is slightly alkaline. Under severe physical tests and hard anaerobic exercise, however, increased acidity can lower the pH level to 6.8 or 6.9. If the pH stays at low levels it can upset the nutritive system, destroying or neutralizing the benefits of vitamins and retarding general development. The pH range within which vitamins function effectively is comparatively small, so any lowering of the level can be deleterious. Under such circumstances, recovery from training is poor and subsequent training is more difficult. The fall in pH level can also affect the central nervous system, causing loss of sleep and irritability, and producing loss of interest in training and competition. It's a physiological reaction that can become seriously psychological.

CARDIAC EFFICIENCY

The two important measures of heart capacity with which we are concerned are *minute volume* (the quantity of blood the heart can pump each minute) and *stroke volume* (the quantity of blood pumped during each contraction). Again, it is a function of my training system to progressively increase both capacities.

Your general efficiency and ultimate results in running depend basically, as we have said, on your ability to absorb oxygen from the air, to transport it to various muscles and organs, and then to utilize it in the operation of muscles and organs. Normally, people take far more oxygen into their lungs than they're able to use because they lack the necessary blood tone to assimilate it. This is due to a deficiency of *hemoglobin*, the pigment in red blood cells that combines with oxygen and transports it. So the aerobic section of the training system is directed toward improving the efficiency of all these factors, separately and collectively.

Through aerobic training, the heart becomes larger and improves its minute and stroke volume. It not only becomes capable of pumping greater quantities of blood with each contraction, but it also pumps faster since increased blood circulation allows it to fill faster. During rest, your heart is able to pump about 4 liters of blood a minute, but it can increase its capacity eight or ten times, according to your condition. An athlete who runs daily for long periods maintains a reasonably high blood pressure in the circulatory system, and steadily develops faster circulation and increased ability to transport greater quantities of blood to various parts of the body.

This harder work and continued pressure bring a steady improvement in *pulmonary ventilation,* the periodic renewal of air in the lungs. The lungs become more efficient because they develop more active pulmonary capillary beds, enabling the blood to absorb oxygen faster and more easily. At the same time, the heart sends greater quantities of blood to the lungs through an improved arterial system, so that the absorption of oxygen into the blood rises markedly and, with it, your ability to use oxygen for exercise.

A consequence of this general improvement is that the heart begins to work more efficiently. This is reflected in a progressive decrease in the basal pulse rate. This rate is influenced by many factors—posture, emotion, body temperature, and exercise—so it is difficult to use it as an exact guide to fitness. It is also misleading for comparisons of athletes because the normal heart rate at rest varies widely, from 50 to 90 beats a minute, from person to person. However, whatever your normal pulse rate, if it is taken while at rest under similar conditions from time to time during training, you will note a steady drop in beats per minute. The rate eventually decreases as much as 25 beats a minute.

Another facet of improved efficiency—circulatory development—has been clearly shown in scientific photographs of muscles. In athletes and manual workers, the arterial network is clearly defined in many well-developed channels for the blood to circulate through. The muscles of sedentary workers, particularly those who don't exercise, show little development, preventing fast and thorough blood circulation. Continued use of the muscles for long periods not only develops underdeveloped capillaries within the muscles, but also new ones. This increases the efficiency with which the muscles can use oxygen and leads to the development of the endurance we seek.

Youngsters of fourteen, fifteen, and even younger who regularly achieve new swimming records are a perfect example of how this theory works in practice. They can outswim mature people to the marks because they do a great deal of aerobic training (long, slow swimming). They couldn't do it if they had to lift their body weight against gravity as runners do. But the buoyancy of the water means they essentially use their muscles solely to propel themselves along. Because their ability to use oxygen efficiently is greater than an adult's in comparison with their body weight, they can manage considerably larger volumes of aerobic exercise. They don't become strong in the sense that they can lift heavy weights. But they are capable of continuing for a long time at comparatively fast swimming speeds without suffering muscle tiredness. This is muscular endurance.

I learned years ago when I was training about 24 kilometers a day that if I shifted the daily balance to 32 kilometers one day and 16 the next, I got better reactions without increasing the total distance I was running. This was simply because the longer runs developed greater muscular endurance, while shorter runs provided both recovery and consolidation.

Years later at Cologne University in West Germany, physiologists experimenting with endurance athletes showed that if muscle groups are exercised continually for long periods—particularly for periods of two hours or more—fine muscular endurance results. They established that this was directly due to the expansion of neglected capillary beds and the formation of new ones.

I am often asked by runners with a daily two-hour program whether it is all right if they split the period into two one-hour sessions. My answer is that *continued* exercise is needed for capillary development, so two short periods will not be nearly as effective as one long one.

This is an argument that long slow distance (LSD) runners sometimes use in favor of their particular approach to training. However, while they will gain from long runs of several hours at a slow pace, they are not going to obtain the finest results. Greater circulatory development will be gained with a higher aerobic pressure than that of LSD training. For best results, aim for a level of 70 to 100 percent of best aerobic effort.

Summing up, athletes, by taking sensible aerobic exercise every day, stimulate their bodies' metabolism into providing progressively richer oxygenated blood, developing:

1. improved absorption of oxygen
2. faster blood circulation from the heart through the arteries, arterioles, capillaries, and veins to the lungs and muscles, and back to the heart
3. more efficient pulmonary ventilation and capillarization, as well as improved utilization of oxygen in the muscles

The quicker the heart can pump blood through the body, the better the performance.

CREATING OXYGEN DEBTS

While aerobic exercise develops general cardiac efficiency and a higher maximum steady state, it is also necessary to develop anaerobic capacity to increase the body's ability to withstand maximum oxygen debts. This means you must create fatigue rates that will stimulate your metabolism to react against them. This metabolic activity can compensate for lack of oxygen up to a limit of about 15 liters. At this level, neuromuscular breakdown—or complete exhaustion—can be withheld until the lactic acid concentration is as high as 200 milligrams to 100 milliliters of blood.

Let us assume a runner has a steady state of 3 liters a minute and can sustain a 15-liter debt. If the workload being performed requires 4 liters a minute, he can maintain the effort for 15 minutes—using 1 liter of his debt capacity each minute. If the workload is increased to 5 liters a minute, he can maintain the effort for only 7.5 minutes—using 2 liters of debt capacity each minute. The oxygen debt doubles, squares, and cubes as the effort increases.

It is essential to understand the extent, intensity, and regularity of these fatigue rates. A lot of training programs are based on this broad principle. But many coaches and athletes go to extremes to create excessive oxygen debts, in the hope that the body's metabolism will be overstimulated to develop more efficiency against fatigue. They try to hurry the process, forgetting that anaerobic exercise is always uneconomical and that when fatigue rates are created, the body must recover before further fatiguing effort is applied.

I've already mentioned that aerobic exercise is nineteen times more economical than anaerobic exercise. It's necessary, therefore, to conserve energy and use it with maximum economy. When the maximum steady state is low, an athlete can run anaerobically at a comparitively easy speed. As the maximum steady state rises, slower anaerobic speeds become aerobic (and economical). And as training progresses on this principle, the possibilities of running farther and faster aerobically—and therefore with economy—increases.

A daily program of sustained running is essential to achieving correct respiratory and circulatory development. The longer the periods of running, the better the results of the sustained effort will be. Running speed, in theory, should be just below your maximum steady state at all times, so you can maintain runs of long duration. Over this level, long-duration running will be beyond you because you will be running anaerobically.

The anaerobic stage of your preparation should only be tackled after you have developed your aerobic capacity and maximum steady state to the highest possible levels. Then it must be fairly extreme for a defined period to develop a matching high anaerobic capacity. At this point, you should aim to create a big oxygen debt and lower the blood pH to stimulate your metabolism to build buffers against fatigue. Once you've built those buffers to maximum efficiency, it's pointless and even risky to go on.

LEVEL OF ANAEROBIC WORK

Four weeks of hard anaerobic training is usually enough. You may need even less. This training involves going hard for, say, three days to lower the blood pH, training lightly for a day to let it return to near normal, and then pulling it down again with anaerobic effort the next day. Let it come up, then pull it down again. Keep it fluctuating. If you keep it low, you upset the entire system.

Continual creation of large oxygen debts accumulates lactic acid and other wastes, upsets the nutritive system, reduces the benefits of vitamins, reduces nourishment from food, disrupts enzyme functions, slows recovery, makes further training difficult, upsets the nervous system, makes you disinterested and irritable, induces insomnia and low spirits, endangers your general health, and makes you vulnerable to injuries and illness.

My most frequent admonition to athletes and coaches is: train, don't strain. Bill Bowerman quoted this phrase in *Coaching Track and Field* to support his LSD principles. But, it applied more accurately to running at faster aerobic speeds than are implied by LSD. East German physiologists have shown that it's better to do long aerobic running at between 70 and 100 percent of your maximum steady state. Lower aerobic effort, while it may be fine for joggers, does not exert the same desirable pressure on the heart and the cardiac and respiratory systems that an athlete needs.

Bowerman also maintains that overtraining can result in staleness and loss of interest in practice and competition, and suggests that the ideal solution is regular competition. I see staleness as a physiological reaction caused by excessive anaerobic work. This becomes psychological through the effects of continual low blood pH on the central nervous system. Lots of competitive racing won't cure that.

I've never noticed athletes who train aerobically over varied courses to lose interest. They do not usually have problems maintaining 160 kilometers a week of fast aerobic running throughout the required conditioning period. When they move into the anaerobic phase, when the physiological problems could again be encountered, they are at a level of cardiac efficiency enabling them to handle the constant fluctuation of blood pH without that staleness side effect.

For a practical example, assume we work with conditioned runner *A* until he has the capacity to use 3 liters of oxygen a minute, and runner *B* up to 5 liters. We then give them the same volume and intensity of anaerobic training. Because his maximum steady state is lower, runner *A* will level off and begin to lose form, fighting a continually larger oxygen debt. Runner *B*, on the other hand, will continue to maintain his best form, since he can use oxygen more effectively and for longer periods. It's easy to see how this physiological effect on runner A can become a psychological problem. He's never going to beat runner B and he can see it.

Let's start these two runners off the same mark in a 1500-meter race. They'll be together at the end of the first lap, and neither will be feeling any strain, since neither has yet experienced the effect of oxygen debt. But, because runner A's capacity to use oxygen is only three-fifths that of runner B, by the time they're into the third lap, A will be feeling the pace. He'll be building an oxygen debt to keep up with runner B, lactic acid will be accumulating, and neuromuscular breakdown will be underway. When runner B fires in his finishing burst, runner A won't be able to answer. And if, by the time they met in this race, runner A's physiological inferiority had also become psychological, he's in real trouble. Which of the two do you want to be?

INTERVAL TRAINING

One of the greatest difficulties I've had in persuading coaches and athletes to accept my system is that the majority are chained to the principles of interval training. They emphasize anaerobic interval training or repetition work as the most important aspect of the training program. As far as I'm concerned, it's the *least* important. Anaerobic capacity can be easily developed to its maximum, without any sort of rigid control, least of all the demanding disciplines of interval training. There is just no need for timing intervals, distance, or the numbers of repetitions run.

The object is simple: to lower blood pH by running into big oxygen debts, to allow blood pH to recover again, and then to lower it once more. This can be done in 101 different ways, since it is only a matter of the athlete becoming tired by hard anaerobic running. He doesn't have to do it by the stern disciplines of running so many times over a certain distance in a particular time.

Before Richard Tayler won the 10,000 meters at the Commonwealth Games in Christchurch in 1974, he and I were working out at a school. The school coach and his athletes were curious to know what times he was running his 400-meter repetitions and how many he was going to run.

"Look," I told them, "he doesn't know and I don't know. It

wouldn't even matter if they weren't 400-meter repetitions. As long as he's tired when he's finished—and he won't stop until he is tired—he's going to get the required physiological reactions."

There is no coach in the world who can say exactly what an athlete should do as far as number of repetitions, distances, and intervals are concerned. Not even physiologists can tell an athlete that. The important point is that the athlete knows what he's trying to achieve and goes out and works at it until he does.

IMPROVED TIMES

Many people have attributed the improved track times in the last decade to improved training techniques or a more enlightened or dedicated approach to training. I wouldn't agree with this. Certainly, there has been a general improvement in the training of athletes throughout the world, but what really brought times down was the introduction of new synthetic tracks. It would have been interesting to see a man like Peter Snell running at his best on them. He would have rebounded off them really fast and could well have set marks that would be difficult to beat today. Remember that he ran his mile, 800-meters, and 880-yards records on grass, which would be at least a second a lap slower than the modern synthetic surfaces—4 seconds in a mile. Compare his 3:54.1 with John Walker's 3:49.4 on that basis, and decide how much—or how little—human improvement has been.

I was in Aarhus, Denmark, in 1972 when the Australian Pam Ryan (nee Kilborn), one of the world's best woman hurdlers, ran there. She had never before run on a synthetic track, and the first time she tried she ran straight into the first hurdle. Pam was noted throughout her career for her fine hurdling and for never hitting hurdles. She told me she didn't realize she would gain so much from the track, and she immediately felt that if she could adjust her approach to the hurdles she could set the world record on a synthetic surface. Three days later, on a synthetic track in Poland, she did exactly that. These tracks are much faster than cinder, clay, grass, or other surfaces.

When synthetic tracks were introduced, the world record for 5,000 meters came down immediately about half a minute, and lots of 10,000-meter runners began running close to and even breaking Ron Clarke's world time. Over the 100 meters, the synthetic surface has been calculated to be worth about 0.2 second.

Although variations in courses make exact comparisons difficult, marathon times haven't improved greatly (though more marathon runners now come close to the best times). It's physiologically possible for a runner with an oxygen uptake level of 6.5 or 7.0 liters—near the human maximum—to run aerobically around 2:12 for a marathon. This is the economic way to run. But if a runner can incur an oxygen debt of up to 15 liters and control his pace to run barely into the anaerobic state for most of the distance so that he ekes out his debt capacity gradually but totally, he can pull that time down to 2:08 or 2:09. Derek Clayton did that about five years ago, and Bill Rodgers did it in 1975. It's more or less the maximum for a human over an out-and-back course without wind or terrain advantages that create deceptively fast times.

This is why marathon running is such a fascinating and demanding sport. A marathon runner must use his anaerobic capacities economically, controlling his running so that he gets just barely into an anaerobic state and stays there. If he runs into it too quickly, he accumulates lactic acid too fast and curtails his possibilities of continuing. This is what most marathon runners do when they run against a superior runner. They match pace with him and run into a big initial oxygen debt and then wonder why they're forced to drift back, why they can't maintain the pace. They'd do better to let the superior runner go and hold a pace at which they can ration out the oxygen debt very slowly. There's always the chance that the superior runner will misjudge his own pace and come back. In a marathon, you're racing to your own capacity as much as anyone else's.

Chapter 2

Marathon Training

My approach to conditioning has changed since the Halberg-Snell era of the early 1960s because I don't often see the athletes I am now coaching. I encourage them to train more on a time basis than on mileage; this has proved the wiser approach for advising at a distance, even for faster athletes. Over, say, a 25-kilometer run, faster runners would not otherwise run as long as a slower athlete so they would miss out on the most important aspect of conditioning—the volume of work they do. In addition, athletes running over a measured course each week are inclined to pressure themselves into becoming more competitive about it. If they go out and run for an hour and a half, anywhere they want to, with less pressure, they seem to get better results. It's important to bear this shift of emphasis in mind while reading this chapter.

If you haven't done marathon conditioning before, you must think deeply about it from the start, and try to understand just what you're trying to achieve. You must relate it to physiological changes, making sure there's no confusion in your mind about the effects of various types of exercise on you. You've got to sort these exercises into their various compartments, balance your schedules, and get rid of any doubts about the approach during each developmental stage, right up to the climax of your racing season. Tackle each stage as a separate exercise, distinct from all others, but with the ultimate target fixed firmly in your mind. Only when you're quite clear about the physiological and mechanical aspects of your training will you develop the confidence you need to become a champion.

The fundamental principle of training is to develop enough stamina to enable you to maintain the necessary speed over the full distance at which you plan to compete. Many runners throughout the world are capable of running 400 meters in 46 seconds or faster. But remarkably few of them have sufficient stamina to run 800 meters in 1:44, or 52 seconds for each 400. That clearly shows the vital part stamina plays in middle- and long-distance racing. Consider those relative times again. It will help you realize what could be achieved by fast runners if they concentrated on endurance development and shifted their attention to longer distances.

Peter Snell was basically the slowest runner in the 800-meter final at both the Rome and Tokyo Olympic Games. But he had the stamina to carry him through the heats and then sprint the last 100 meters of the finals faster than any of his rivals. By then they were too tired to use their superior speed. Snell was trained to be capable of running a fine marathon, but I doubt that his rivals could. This was the advantage that enabled him to succeed; it's also the advantage you can give yourself.

BUILDING STAMINA

Quite simply, it means putting your body into a near-tireless state so that oxygen debts are not created quickly and the ability to recover rapidly is at a high level. Stamina is general cardiac efficiency and the best way to develop it other than cross-country skiing is by running. That running is best done at just under your maximum steady state, for approximately 160 kilometers a week. This is quite apart from any easier supplementary running, such as jogging, that you feel inclined to do.

In our first book, we based the stamina-building phase on 160 kilometers a week of aerobic running. This led many runners to believe it was a rigid requirement. In this connection, an Australian doctor with an interest in sports medicine mentioned to me that the 160 kilometers I advocated was insufficient, and that Australian athletes were running 320 kilometers a week. He didn't understand, perhaps because we didn't explain it comprehensively enough, just what my athletes were doing. They were running 160 kilometers a week at their near-best aerobic effort during their evening runs and on a long-duration weekend run.

But they, like the Australians, were also covering several more kilometers in supplementary morning and midday training sessions during which the pace was considerably easier. My middle-distance men—Snell and John Davies at that time—were running the lowest weekly mileages, but even they were totalling around 250 kilometers a week.

I asked the Australian doctor, as a physiologist, if he believed it was possible for a runner to train more than 160 kilometers a week for periods of months at top aerobic speeds. He couldn't answer because he didn't know. But I knew that no runner could do it. For years, I ran many kilometers trying to find the correct balance for my conditioning training. I knew you could both undertrain and overtrain in both mileage and effort. I ran from extremes of 80 to 500 kilometers a week at close to my best aerobic effort. And when I added the slower-speed supplementary runs at other times of the day, I found that they assisted my recovery from the long aerobic effort and hastened the rate of my development.

Running is without question the best exercise for runners and, provided you watch the degree of effort, you can't really do too much of it. Certain physiologists have said that unless the pulse rate is brought up to 150-80 beats a minute, the athlete gains very little cardiac development. This is absolutely wrong. I have never believed it. If an athlete with a normal pulse rate of 50 to 60 lifts the rate to 100, he will get cardiac development. So *all* supplementary jogging, while it may not impose the pressure on the system to the degree that near maximum steady-state running does, affords extra benefits to the cardiac system, as well as aiding the athlete's recovery.

The long steady running that I term marathon training is designed to create a state of fatigue, though not so great as to interfere with the next day's program. You should be able to recover reasonably quickly.

DETERMINING YOUR CAPABILITY

First you have to find your own basic capability. The best way to do this is to run an out-and-back course for, say, 30 minutes. Run out for 15 minutes at a steady pace; then turn and run back again, trying to maintain that pace without forcing yourself. If it takes you 20 minutes to get back, it shows you've run the outward leg too fast for your condition. If you're back inside 15 minutes without apparently increasing your effort, you haven't run fast enough to begin with. Next time, you should adjust your pace according to your insights about your condition and capability, so that you return in the same time as the outward journey. It's good discipline, and that's something you have to acquire early because you're going to need a lot of it later on.

As you learn more about yourself and improve your general physical condition, you'll be able to run both farther and faster. But you should understand that it's the speed of the running that stops you, not the distance. Running that breaks the even passage of time and distance is anaerobic, not aerobic, and it must be avoided. It's much better to go too slowly at first than too fast. If you can recognize that as important and discipline yourself to it, you're on the way to becoming a greater runner than you believed possible.

MARATHON TRAINING SCHEDULES

For psychological reasons, you should train by time rather than mileage at first. This keeps you from translating your efforts into comparisons with the four-minute mile. Vary your runs from 15 to 30 minutes for a period, forgetting all about the kilometers you're tucking behind you. You should increase this rapidly until you can follow this kind of schedule (for adults):

Monday	1 hour
Tuesday	1½ hours
Wednesday	1 hour
Thursday	2 hours
Friday	1 hour
Saturday	2-3 hours
Sunday	1½ hours

All this running must be steady and even, at a pace that leaves you tired at the end, but knowing you could have run faster if you'd wanted to. In other words, you should be pleasantly tired.

Most athletes doubt that they can run long distances day after day or even for an hour or more without stopping, particularly when they feel extremely tired during the initial short-duration runs. It's a hurdle you must overcome if you want to improve.

In only a few weeks, with patience, you'll find that what had seemed impossible is becoming progressively easier and more enjoyable. Just don't rush it. Once you're moving freely over the shorter runs, you should move into one or two longish runs each week to maintain the improvement rate and build confidence in yourself. Then you'll find it easy to slide into the schedule outlined above.

Once you've mastered that schedule, or one similar to it, you can move on to one that concerns itself more with distance than time, and progressively increase your speed as your maximum steady state rises and your muscles and general condition become stronger:

Monday	15 kilometers at one-half effort over an undulating course
Tuesday	25 kilometers at one-fourth effort over a reasonably flat course
Wednesday	20 kilometers at one-half effort over a hilly course
Thursday	30 kilometers at one-fourth effort over a reasonably flat course
Friday	15 kilometers at three-fourths effort over a flat course
Saturday	35 kilometers at one-fourth effort over a reasonably flat course
Sunday	25 kilometers at one-fourth effort over any type of terrain

Several courses should have been measured for this training, with each kilometer marked, so you can time yourself with reasonable accuracy. They should not, however, be viewed as kilometer pegs in a race.

MARATHON TRAINING TECHNIQUE

In theory, you're now doing a lot of your running at speeds just within your maximum steady state. This places the utmost, aerobic *safe* pressure on your heart from the cardiorespiratory and cardiovascular systems, and offers the best possible progressive development. You should run over each of your measured courses at your best steady rate of speed—hard but evenly—but still finish with the knowledge that you could have run a little faster.

Your aim is to find your best aerobic speed over the various courses. If, during any of these runs, you find you have to ease back a little to recover, you'll know that you've moved into the anaerobic phase. This is neither economical nor desirable. You could go on running your courses anaerobically and quite evenly for several days, but then you would find yourself unable to continue because of the gradual breakdown of your whole system. So take careful note of any early warning signs and move your speed back if necessary. Once you've established approximately the best aerobic effort for each course, you can cover successive runs. Try to maintain a strong, even pace all the way, at previously planned times.

This way, it becomes possible to maintain the utmost economical pressure on the cardiac system without creating excessive waste products in the body that could slow progress and dishearten you. As your maximum steady state rises, the runs over the courses will become progressively faster, and you'll be working aerobically at speeds that earlier would have been anaerobic— or even impossible.

Running, I repeat, is the best exercise for runners, and the more you do in a balanced aerobic-anaerobic ratio according to this overall system, the better you'll be. Conditioning running helps to develop strong upper-leg muscles, which are the only ones powerful enough to make the heart work at the effort and for the lengths of time necessary to gain the desired results. The longer and more steadily you use those big muscles to lift your body against gravity, the better. With this in mind, jumping and skipping in addition to your daily runs are also beneficial.

Experience has shown me that runners who train for marathons at steady aerobic speeds improve in general condition faster and better than runners using interval training, which is basically anaerobic. This is directly attributable to the steady, sustained pressure on the circulatory and respiratory systems from marathon training, as opposed to the irregular extremes of pressure involved in interval training. The fact that the marathon system reduces the accumulation of waste products in the body is also highly relevant. The marathon training method works best for the circulatory, respiratory, and nervous systems.

The marathon-training runner covers far more kilometers in his hour of training than the interval-training runner. In addition, he applies the steady pressure on his cardiac system required for the development of stamina, while the interval man merely creates excessive oxygen debt by subjecting himself to a series of sustained pressures.

You may have been under the impression that marathon training involves slow running. Apart from the supplementary work, this isn't so. World-class runners don't jog around in this phase of their preparation, but run at speeds of from 3.75 minutes to 3.25 minutes per kilometer. There are still some long-distance runners who believe they should run only at a 4.25-minute pace, and that to run faster wastes effort and produces poorer results. Again, this isn't so. Runners who keep their speed just within their maximum steady state gain the same general cardiac development in far less time as runners who train at speeds far below the maximum steady state.

However, it is important to bear in mind that no two of us are the same. The guidelines I set our here should be treated flexibly, according to the fitness level and age of the individual. Don't let age deter anyone from tackling long mileages, as long as the individual is happy about it and exercises carefully.

We have been overly cautious about allowing very young people to run long distances. But we now know that, provided they are not pushed along, but are allowed to settle into a comfortable speed or level of effort, they can cover many miles easily and beneficially. There are cases of boys ten to twelve running up to 160 kilometers a week and continuing to improve. No one can say exactly what the limits are for the individual. It's a question of each runner adjusting to running and doing what he likes, on the basic understanding that the more he runs aerobically, the better the prospects for development. We'll look at the young runner's requirements in more detail later.

Black Africans have emerged as remarkably successful runners, simply because running is part of their everyday lives. Many of them became runners because they had many kilometers to cover on foot to and from school, and the quickest way was to run. Although this is not controlled running, it is a vital form of training, and it has laid the foundation for their future development as good racers. They have lived closer to nature and developed better muscular and cardiac efficiency quite early. They became superior because, without really knowing it or working at it, they were doing more conditioning exercising. We let our kids sit back in buses and cars between home and school, while the Africans get there and back by running.

In 1961, the Victorian cross-country team came to New Zealand for competition, and performed so badly that they asked my athletes what was wrong. It was explained to them that they should follow our system of long marathon running, with less anaerobic work. Two of the Victorians, Vincent and Cook, returned to Australia and began longer marathon running. They trained with other athletes, including Ron Clarke, who had retired from running two years earlier but had decided to make a comeback. Clarke had previously trained on an interval program, with lots of hard anaerobic track work.

Four years later I was in Saarijarvi, Finland, when Clarke arrived for a 3,000-meter race. One of my runners, John Davies, who had won the 1,500-meter bronze medal in Tokyo, was also competing. Davies had never raced the distance before, but, since he was marathon-trained, I was confident he could run it well, even with the well-conditioned Clarke in the field. I advised him to trail Ron until the last 150 meters. I felt he could beat Clarke from there. But I also felt that by the time Clarke found he could not get rid of Davies, due to his inferior speed, he would have already mentally given away the race long before. That's what happened; John beat Ron quite easily in 7:58. In Czechoslovakia, two weeks later, over the same distance, Davies comfortably beat the reigning Olympic 5,000-meter champion, Bob Schul, in 7:52. Each race was a convincing demonstration of the value of marathon-trained stamina in combination with speed development.

After the Saarijarvi race, Clarke asked me why he had showed so badly against Davies, why he had no speed, no kick to counter Davies's speed at the finish. I asked what he'd been doing in training, and found that, from 1961, he'd joined Cook and Vincent in long-distance running at a 7-minute mile pace. He'd become fitter and felt the benefit of this running until, while Cook, Vincent, and the others continued at the same speed, he felt he should run faster. As his steady state improved, he began putting in mileages that he had never attempted before. By the time of the 1962 British Empire and Commonwealth Games in Perth,

The 5,000-meter final at the 1964 Tokyo Olympics. The runners are (left to right): Bill Dellinger (U.S.), Kip Keino (Kenya), Bob Schul (U.S.), Bill Baillie (New Zealand), Nicolai Dutov (USSR), Harold Norpoth (W. Germany), Ron Clarke (Australia), and Michael Jazy (France). (Photograph by Mark Shearman.)

he was fit enough to run second in the 3 miles to Murray Halberg.

However, Clarke, while doing the right thing in continuing to increase his running speed as his maximum steady state increased, didn't carry the program through to the proper conclusion to take fullest advantage of his development. He was running faster and more economically as he got fitter. But his program lacked the necessary anaerobic and sprint training that would have balanced it and given his running the vital edge. On my advice he began to do some repetition training on the track, thus increasing his ability to exercise and race anaerobically. This capitalized on his otherwise excellent general condition so effectively that, soon after the Saarijarvi race, he set world records for the 6 miles and 10,000 meters in Oslo.

Clarke is a good early example of an athlete who failed to improve solely with interval training, and became tired of training by this hard and unrewarding method. But once he began training aerobically, he discovered that he not only improved but enjoyed his training for the first time, and didn't wish to revert to the type of training that had failed him before. But he didn't understand that he still needed the tough anaerobic work to sharpen him up.

I believe Ron is the best distance runner the world has seen, but he did not balance his schedules. This was why he failed in the important competitions. He proved that it's not always the best athletes who win the big ones; it's the best-prepared ones, those who are completely ready on the vital day.

During the conditioning stage, athletes of all types should differentiate between the development and toning of the cardiac and muscular systems. Only by forcing body weight against gravity, using the powerful upper-leg muscles, can you make the heart work hard for long periods. Fortunately, runners actually use all the muscles required for their sport during this conditioning stage, since they use running for most of their exercising. Therefore, it is only necessary to do suppling and loosening exercises at every opportunity to round out the development. This shouldn't involve any sacrifice of running time.

TRAINING ON ROADS

The surfaces you choose to run on are important. The better the traction from the surface, the better the development of the circulatory and respiratory systems. Good traction allows more economical running, which, in turn, allows greater speed for longer periods within the maximum steady state.

Most of my runners trained on bitumen roads for better traction. We tested this by having an athlete run for an hour cross-country and comparing that with the distance he could run in an hour on the road. On the road, he covered a much greater distance without any increase of effort, solely because he had better traction and could move more economically. As a result, the muscles tire less. In cross-country, the muscles tire faster because of the continued resistance of uphill and downhill running on slippery, wet, or holding ground, where traction is bad. This is muscular, not cardiac, fatigue. On the road, even when there are hills to run up and down, the runner has good traction and can run much more relaxed. Though general fatigue may be greater, it is no problem as long as he is running within his steady state. In fact, fatigue helps him, since sustained pressure is the best developer of the general circulatory system.

Many athletes and coaches avoid training on roads. But if you use well-made shoes with good rubber soles, the risk of injuries or leg problems is less than that involved in running with ordinary track shoes on hard cinder tracks.

LEG SORENESS

In your first year of marathon training, you are likely to get leg soreness, particularly about the knees and shins. Usually, if training is continued carefully, the soreness is overcome. If it persists, seek medical opinion. When you experience soreness, avoid jarring the legs too much. Don't run down hills fast, seek out softer surfaces for training, and keep the affected areas warm.

Shin soreness usually stems from overstriding or running downhill too fast. Both actions cause the front of the foot to clap down hard, jarring the shin muscles and causing irritation to the nerves and membranes between the bone and the muscles. In some cases, the muscle sheaths split.

This problem can be overcome by shortening your stride and eliminating fast downhill running from your program. It's not easy, however. Once you've developed shin soreness, it can take quite a while to recover. If you are a long-striding runner and susceptible to shin splints, it is better to avoid overstriding and running downhill too fast. You can also build up the forepart of your shoes with an extra half-sole of rubber to reduce the element of foot clap.

For all leg troubles, wading in cold water is excellent. It will often effect a cure where other methods fail. Ice packs also help.

All runners can expect some initial troubles. But they can be overcome if common sense and professional advice is used. Most of the world's greatest athletes have had setbacks and recovered from them.

UPPER BODY AND LEG ACTION

During conditioning running, always try to relax, particularly the upper body. Keep the head up and the hips comfortably forward; this allows you to stride longer and more economically. Never waste energy.

Try to keep your arm action low. Runners with a high arm action aren't relaxed and tend to throw their torsos from side to side. They don't get over their driving legs and lose some forward momentum. Test yourself by running on sand and then checking your footprints. If you're running balanced, your feet should fall directly one behind the other; if you're not, they'll vary either side of a straight centerline. If they're unbalanced, you'll lose forward motion.

I don't belong to the clenched-fist or air-clutching school of studied stylists. The late Hec Hogan, the Australian sprinter and former co-world record-holder, was my mirror of the perfect running action. He was fully relaxed, even under extreme pressure, with arms driving straight through and carried easily at a natural height. The minute you clench your fists you tense arm and shoulder muscles, and encourage swaying and loss of balance. Tensed muscles also waste energy.

Don't run on your toes. This works calf muscles unnaturally, which is uncomfortable and tiring over long distances. It is most economical and natural to come down with a nearly flat foot, with the heel hitting first and a slight roll in from the outside edge of the foot. There are many good runners who run on their toes, but I contend they would run better still, in distance work, with a nearly flat footfall.

In the 800 meters or less, of course, you should run on your toes, as the sprinter naturally does when he throws his body forward and stretches out his stride. But before you get to that point you should be conditioned to do it.

There are some runners who appear to have rather tight or short tendons in the backs of their legs that prevent them from running heel to toe when running aerobically. When the forward momentum is such that the center of gravity is slow getting forward of the leading foot, there is resistance to the front of the foot that is not experienced in the heel-to-toe rolling action. These runners often have foot problems, caused by friction during high-volume aerobic running, resulting in blisters and metatarsal injury. They should try to keep the movement of their feet in their shoes to a minimum by lacing shoes tightly, and rubbing lubricant onto their feet to reduce friction.

There is no set rule for how you breathe. You'll consume a great amount of oxygen while you are running and it doesn't matter how you get it. You can't drag in enough through the nose, although some European coaches have insisted that you not only can but should. I don't care how wide open your mouth is. And I hold no brief with the old extended rhythm system developed by the Finns, beginning with four strides to the inhale and two to the exhale and increasing until there are up to eight strides on the inhale and six on the exhale. They used to practice this assidu-ously, but I feel that something artificial or unnatural is being built in and that it could react against the essential relaxation, the runner's first requirement. You'll pant and need to gulp in liters of oxygen while you are running. But don't worry about how you get it, or how you look while you're getting it. If you must, open your mouth wide and use it.

In marathon training running, concentration on technicalities like center of gravity can cause awkwardness. If you move with a balanced, easy stride, free of unnecessary swing and sway, you'll adjust your body position comfortably. The long-legged runner naturally tends to lean forward to accommodate to the longer stride; the short man with the springy stride tends to lean back. Each should run with a comfortable balance, and hips forward. A good tip is to fasten your eyes straight ahead to a point about 60 meters away.

Leg action is governed by body lean. Backward lean exaggerates the knee-lift while forward lean emphasizes the back kick. Both waste energy, but can be remedied naturally if the body is at a relaxed angle. There are exceptions to all this, and high knee lift is encouraged later in building in speed. It's all a matter of the individual's build.

I don't try to stretch the length of an athlete's stride by encouraging him to stride out between measured pegs. When a runner is fit and running well, he will reach out automatically, always striking a length that conforms to his build and running development. Long, leggy runners stride long, while big chunky types like Snell gain length from a natural bounding or bouncing action. Halberg had a shortish stride, with a characteristic flicking action of the leg, enabling him to stride fast. He had good leg speed. Stride length will develop naturally as fitness grows, and as you move into hill training and other phases of the program that add spring to the natural leg movement without strain or deliberate concentration.

I favor the low-swinging arm action, with the thumbs skimming the seams of the shorts. This keeps them moving straight through and guides balance—the essential value of arm action. Arms don't assist the distance runner much, apart from aiding balance, and the low action is natural, relaxed, and automatic. It takes energy to hold the arms up high. Halberg was a case in point. His withered arm became a trademark around the world and was perhaps the finest example of how little a physical disability of this kind need handicap a runner. It also showed how little arms affect good running. Halberg was probably one of the most relaxed and balanced runners in the world.

Snell was no stylist. He had an awkward motion, seeming to lumber and roll until he began pace running. He did not really seem balanced properly until he began running under 55 seconds for the quarter, but he was always comfortably relaxed. It would not have helped him to adjust his body position or eliminate his tendency to roll slightly.

So, if you want to run well on the track, begin by running on the road—long, relaxed, easy running, pushing up your maximum steady state, building endurance and stamina. It's the first and most important ingredient of the program. Vary the daily rations, but work toward the guideline of 160 kilometers a week. If you have time—and, if you want to be a champion, you will—do supplementary jogging during other daily sessions, as well as suppling and loosening exercises. If you go about the preliminary buildup quietly, steadily, and, above all, patiently, you'll be surprised how soon you'll be able to run apparently large mileages, and how comfortably you'll continue the program.

Olympic 5,000-meter champ Murray Halberg lining up for a heat at the Olympics. (Photograph by Mark Shearman.)

Chapter 3

Anaerobic Training

This phase begins after the marathon running conditioning period, but you should keep it in mind right through the initial conditioning. You should allow for it by consistently doing resistance work for the leg muscles, and by stretching your tendons for flexibility and suppleness to add to your power. Some hill springing and steep hill running should be worked into the marathon conditioning period as an added incentive to the development of the upper leg muscles.

As you come to the end of the marathon running and cross-country conditioning, you should have good stamina and be well toned. This will ready you for development of speed and help increase your capacity to exercise anaerobically, two elements in the program we have been deliberately avoiding until now.

Some of you are fortunate enough to have certain natural talents that give you advantages in different areas; good basic speed can be one of those talents. Since this is a governing factor for running specific distances, you must determine your basic speed before making the decision about what events to concentrate on. Before this point, it isn't important to make this decision, because you weren't fit enough to test yourself accurately. And regardless of whether you decide to run 800s or 10,000s, the marathon conditioning program is exactly the same.

No one can make a basically slow runner into a fast runner, although better speed can be developed to a limited extent by muscular toning and an improvement in general condition and technique. Whatever you do, basically slow runners will remain relatively slow. This doesn't mean they'll never win races. If they choose distances at which lack of sprint speed doesn't matter, they can, through proper training, become champions. I refer you again to my comments on Snell's slow basic speed in relation to most other 800-meter runners and his end results.

MUSCLE DEVELOPMENT

Muscles contain a number of fibers—some red, others white. The red fibers contain *myoglobin,* which is chemically related to hemoglobin in the blood. Muscles in which these fibers predominate are capable of slow, powerful contractions and are not easily fatigued. The white muscle fibers contain less myoglobin and are specialized for speed, not strength, so they tire much more easily.

Runners with a good basic speed appear to have a higher than normal ratio of white muscle fibers to red, and this is one reason for their advantage. The quantity and ratio of red and white fibers you're born with remains the same, although, with exercise and resistance, the fibers will become larger and generally more efficient.

There are many informative books about the development and toning of various muscles. For a better understanding of the subject, I recommend that athletes read some of them. (See the Bibliography.)

There are two kinds of muscle contraction—*isometric* and *isotonic.* The contraction is isotonic when the muscular effort results in movement, such as lifting, pushing, or pulling something that moves. It is isometric when force is applied by pushing, pulling, or trying to lift an immovable object. Both forms of resistance have value in exercise, so athletes and coaches should evaluate and apply them to specific needs.

I discovered that if I gave certain muscles work to perform, similar to the eventual exercise that I wanted them to do, I gained fine results. When speed development is the aim, you should concentrate on the white muscle fibers. In sprinting, these muscles are required to work for a short period in a series of short, sharp contractions. Therefore, they require exercise that allows for quick resistance pressures in a series of repetitions that aren't too fatiguing, but are sufficient to impel all the fibers to work. I found that an isotonic exercise is best, and that springing up hills is an isotonic exercise similar to the movement needed in the eventual competition.

Fundamentally, speed is developed in two ways: through longer strides and a faster stride frequency. To develop longer strides, you have to increase the power and flexibility of the legs. Increased stride frequency will come with greater reflex actions, better coordination, and more flexibility, relaxation, and technique. Applying resistance to the muscles to increase the size and strength of the fibers will help achieve strength.

It is important, in all types of running, to have strong quadriceps to maintain good knee-lift throughout the entire distance. Knee-lift is relative to the speed at which you are running. Though a marathon runner shouldn't keep the knees high during a race, he should run with his knees at a height that gives him the most economical stride length and frequency. A sprinter, however, must bring his knees up high, not only because it lengthens his stride, but because it brings his feet through high and fast.

I have seen many 400-meter runners drop their knees over the last 50 meters, as their upper bodies tightened, and their legs began to waver because their quadriceps were not strong enough to maintain good knee-lift. So many of them lose their speed that I've been saying for years that a lot of 400-meter runners are really good 300-meter runners. They stagger the last 50 to 100 meters because they haven't conditioned themselves to continue the high knee drive to the finish line. All the power drains from their running once they hit the home straight. If it can happen so easily over 400 meters, you can imagine what it must be like over longer distances.

Run regularly on steep hills to activate the upper leg muscles. Work until your muscles feel the exercise, and keep at it steadily. Suppling and loosening exercises should also be done on a regular basis at this stage, with particular attention to ankle flexibility. Too many runners have inefficient ankle action. Look at the ankles of gymnasts and ballet dancers, and you'll realize what great ankle flexibility can be attained. The increased striding efficiency is worth the little effort.

DETERMINING BASIC SPEED

Through this speed buildup, watch your technique carefully. You should run balanced and relaxed, and maintain an economical stride length. As you get into speed development, you should do a sprint to find out your basic speed. Run it over 200 meters rather than 100 because your start can affect the time of a 100-meter sprint. Beyond 200 meters, stamina is required, and this can also influence the result.

As far as I'm concerned, this sprint test is the best way to judge your potential. Your basic speed—not your build, leg length, or weight—should determine what distance you run. If you can't run the 200 faster than 26 seconds, for instance, forget all about half-miling. All the training in the world won't make you a champion at it. Halberg's best 200 was about 25 seconds. To run 800 in 1:52, he ran flat out all the way, and near his best sprinting speed. He just couldn't run any faster. However his stamina was such that, soon after running one 800 that fast, he could run another just as fast again. Though he could run at nearly his basic speed over distances twelve times as long, he could never have become a great 800-meter runner.

A man who can run 22.5 for 200 is basically fast enough to become an Olympic 800-meter champion, if he has the stamina. While George Kerr could run the 200 in 21 seconds, he lacked the stamina to keep running fast all the way. Snell, who ran the 200 in 22.3, was almost tireless at the distance. Roger Moens, who ran second in the Rome 800, and Snell were the slowest 200-meter men in the field, but both were stamina men. Even after the preliminaries, they could continue running at near their basic speed. Speedsters without stamina didn't have a chance against them as long as the overall pace was maintained.

If you can barely break a minute for 400 meters, you can't hope to succeed over 800 meters, no matter what you do. If you can't run a 400 in 51 seconds, you can't run an 800 in 1:50. And if you can't do that, you don't have a chance in today's racing circles. But if you can do the 400 in under 51 seconds, you can build in the stamina to maintain that running speed and become a fine 800-meter runner.

Athletes and coaches often do not appreciate the significance and permanence of basic speed. As a result, many runners are given distances they'll never master, and running soon sours on them. One of New Zealand's first great half-milers, Doug Harris, plugged away for years as a run-of-the-mill sprinter. Then, when he started to be beaten, he switched to the half-mile, and New Zealand discovered it had a world-class runner. He could have run a 4-minute mile when others were still dreaming of it, but unfortunately he was spiked and forced out of the sport before he could gain the recognition he deserved.

This doesn't mean that a sprint champion would necessarily make a middle-distance champion. But many potential sprint champions would actually make better middle-distance men, since their lack of basic speed gives them a disadvantage before they even start sprinting.

You can classify runners still more closely, into pullers and drivers, depending on how they run. *Pullers* skim the ground with little physical effort, and usually make ideal cross-country runners. *Drivers* have a comparatively labored style and have trouble on rough or soft ground. This is because they have to drive harder to maintain speed, thus accelerating their exhaustion rate. Ireland's Ron Delaney was a typical driver, hunched up and visibly forcing himself along with every stride. He didn't look relaxed. Halberg was a puller; he just drifted along.

The relaxation and economy of movement in Barry Magee's running convinced me long before he thought of racing the marathon that he would have success at that distance. He was the embodiment of conservation of effort, a ballet dancer of the road in the way he floated along. He could run 65 kilometers without feeling tired; his endless glide was completely natural. The only thing I take credit for is recognizing his gift, and helping him find the distance for which he was best suited. I prepared the schedule that ran him to the top, and that would have kept him there if persistent leg trouble hadn't forced him to quit.

Age is another factor dictating your performance. You cannot be hurried into your best distance. For instance, a natural 3-miler should be mature enough at twenty-five to produce his best running, but he should not be discouraged if he is still short of championship times at twenty-two. It was this that led me to predict that Halberg would emerge as the world's best long before he did.

Snell was a champion at twenty-two, and had it within him then to be the greatest runner ever at the mile and 1,500 meters, his true distances. I still believe the quality of his running has not been bettered. When we first wrote *Run to the Top,* I predicted that a 3:47 mile, a 1:44 half-mile, a 13-minute 3 miles, and a 27-minute 6 miles were all within reach of runners then in action. Snell hit that 1:44 only two years later with a remarkable solo run on a grass track.

Magee, Halberg, and Snell all used their respective basic speeds to best advantage. It is important in your running to discover your own basic speed so that you can begin setting targets with some prospect of achieving real success.

TRAINING FOR SPEED

You're now at the stage of training when your maximum steady state is as high as possible. This means you're ready to accustom yourself to exercising anaerobically, incorporating small quantities of anaerobic running into your schedule, and progressively increasing both the volume and intensity. This, like most other phases, is time-consuming, so you should avoid unnecessary exercises. This is a period for developing speed, power, suppleness, technique, and increasing your capacity to exercise anaerobically.

We are all busy with school or work, so training time has its limits. Since we can't do all the necessary running and other essential activities separately, we have to combine the exercises. If we do this right, we not only save time, we can achieve results. These can be just as good as if we'd used weight training for power development, calisthenics and gymnastics to improve suppleness and speed, running training to upgrade technique, and further running to add to anaerobic capacity. My schedules combine all these aspects of training within each session.

Always bear in mind that the wise only train according to their age, physical condition, and their capacity to exercise. They learn quickly about themselves and train by that knowledge, increasing volume and intensity only when they feel their condition has improved. If you train and race fast too soon, without proper consideration of the various aspects of training, you are doomed to disappointment. You must understand what you are attempting and what effects your exercising will have.

Feel your way along patiently and do only what you feel capable of doing at each stage of the training session. The schedules in this book are only guides to what is desirable. They can be amended and the work load reduced and still produce excellent results. This is better than forcing yourself to train too hard, always to the limits. The training I outline here is exacting and initially difficult, and only dogged perseverance will enable you to become used to it. Tackle it with common sense and caution, and within a couple of weeks you'll find it more manageable.

HILL TRAINING

Try to find a hill at least 300 meters long, rising at a gradient of near one in three, on a road, in the country, or on a forest trail, with 400 to 800 meters of reasonably flat ground at both top and bottom. The best alternative is a circuit with a smallish, steep hill for uphill work, a less steep hill for downhill running, and flattish areas both top and bottom between them for speed training and jogging. When you begin training on this hill circuit, run first at warming-up speed for about 2 kilometers. If temperatures permit, unnecessary clothing should be discarded to allow freedom of movement—most important in this phase of training.

At the base of the steeper hill, start springing up, on your toes, not running up, but bouncing. You must lift and drop the center of gravity, using your body weight as a form of resistance to the leg muscles. This gives you muscular development and flexibility through the extreme actions of the legs in first driving upward with a high knee-lift, and then taking the force of your body weight as it comes down again. Drive hard, pushing upward with your toes, flexing your ankles as far as possible and landing on the forepart of your foot. The heel should come down below the level of the toe as the weight is taken. This action stretches the calf muscles both upward and downward as far as possible. It also applies resistance, thoroughly exercising muscle fibers, so that flexibility and power are added simultaneously to build an economical stride length.

If you want to develop fast strides or increase stride frequency, your feet will have to follow through as close to the buttocks as possible. If you move your feet through close to the ground, it will result in a much slower stride. But you can't bring your feet through with a high action unless you run with your hips farther forward. Some of the world's best sprinters run with a seemingly backward-leaning action. While this action should not be exaggerated, you must lean such that foot strike is comfortable, economical, and makes for fast leg action.

Concentrate on running with your head up and looking straight ahead. If your head falls forward, your hips will tend to be held back. They should be sufficiently forward to allow the knees to rise high, which in turn allows the feet to follow through high. If your hips are back, there is no way you can get your knees up high enough.

I've watched athletes running with their hips back, with a distinct forward lean, and their heels kicking up high in back. They seem to be running into the ground. Their body attitude forces them to run with a short stride, preventing them from running faster. I've seen athletes struggling to hold the lead in a middle-distance race when, simply by shifting their hips forward, they could lengthen stride, reduce effort, and maintain a faster pace. This is not a question of conditioning; it is simply a matter of technique.

As you spring up that hill, your arms, shoulders, neck, and facial muscles should be relaxed. Keep your head up and looking ahead, with hips slightly forward, and legs driving down forcefully. Push hard with the toes, raise the knees high, and then apply body-weight resistance to the leg muscles as your feet hit the ground. Your progression up the hill will be gradual, not fast. Do only as much hill springing as your condition allows, and only increase the work load as your muscles become accustomed to it.

At the top, take a recovery period by jogging easily. You should not stop running. When you hit the downward hill, you should run fast, with relaxed, slightly longer strides. With no resistance against them, your muscles will be able to recover further, and you will feel stretching in the legs, the stomach muscles, and the hips. You should do some exercises for your stomach muscles to make them more supple for easier breathing when you're running under pressure, with your heart and lungs expanded. Unless your stomach muscles are supple, you'll apply pressure to your diaphragm, pulling at the ligaments that attach the diaphragm to the bone. This results in stomach cramps or stitches, the sharp pains that can force you to stop or ease up.

The downhill running tends to throw the body backward a little further, stretching your stomach muscles and increasing pressure on the diaphragm. You can help offset this by doing backward-bending exercises as muscle stretchers. If you use a road for this training, it is imperative to wear shoes with thick rubber soles and heels, not shoes with the heel cut away.

ANAEROBIC TRAINING

At the foot of the hill, use the flat section for sprint repetitions, varying them with each circuit you run. In these repetitions, use whatever distances, from 50 to 400 meters, you feel are best suited for you, although, for best results, you should try to put in 50-, 100-, 200-, and 400-meter runs during the training sessions. If the circuit is short, do wind sprints only every 15 minutes. These sprint repetitions begin development of your capacity to exercise anaerobically. This is the culmination of all the work you've been doing to lift your maximum steady state as high as possible and to develop good oxygen transportation to cope with the work overload and the resulting metabolic upsets. If you're well conditioned, your body will adjust very quickly to anaerobic training, as long as you keep the intensity at reasonable levels.

Even if you are well conditioned, it is not advisable to suddenly do intense anaerobic training, as many athletes do. Just as you carefully built the aerobic steady state, you must carefully raise the capacity to exercise anaerobically without sacrificing any of that condition. You must guard that condition carefully, as it is the foundation on which you build all your future strengths.

You should confine the anaerobic work in these training sessions to the repetitions you can accomplish within a flat stretch of only 600 to 800 meters. The benefit will accrue gradually, but sufficiently, without creating too much waste product. Every stage of training must be approached in this same gradual way. You must allow your body to accustom itself to the various forms of exercise.

You'll rapidly feel the effects of the initial anaerobic work. You'll have a burning sensation in your throat and other immediate effects, as you shift into speed work after the longer, slower road running and cross-country work you've been doing. You'll become aware of the benefit week after week, as your ability to handle the work becomes greater and the effort easier. Do it thoroughly and sensibly, and by the time you get onto the track, you'll be well prepared to handle the increased volume and intensity of the repetitions and interval work that follow.

A mature runner in good condition should spend about an hour on the hill circuit session, apart from the warming up and cooling down periods, which should take about 15 minutes each. If you're a woman, a girl, a youth, or a mature man who is a novice to this type of training, limit the work according to your capacity. The exercises are most valuable if you tackle them sensibly and patiently, not to excess.

If you haven't got a hill to run on, don't despair. You can do the hill springing work on flat ground. The resistance from the body weight will still be reasonably effective on the leg muscles, although the flexing of the ankles won't be as marked. You can supplement your training by standing on a raised object, such as a book or block, on the front of your feet. Lift yourself up and down, allowing the heels to fall well below the level of the stand. Or you may find a stadium or some other building with steps or stairs on which you can do the springing exercises. The downhill striding would have to be equalled by doing relaxed, fast striding, with an exaggerated stride action.

Next time around the circuit, you can vary the training by running up a steep hill with a high knee-lift, to place most of the work on the quadriceps or front upper-leg muscles. The next time around again, you can run uphill, pushing mostly with the ankles, while lifting the knees. Then return to the hill springing. All the leg muscles, including the quadriceps, benefit from this training.

Another valuable exercise for this phase is frog hopping, with or without the addition of resistance weights. Go right down on your haunches and spring in hops for 50 to 100 meters. You must get low and spring high, returning to your haunches each time. A bag of sand on your shoulders will add resistance; it's better than holding weights as you jump, because it doesn't upset the balance.

The hill circuit program lasts six weeks. During this period, you should spend three days a week on the hill, alternating with three days of leg-speed running and one of long-distance running. I originally had my athletes spend more time on the hill work, but I've found that some runners become quite dejected trying to maintain this pressure for the whole period. This was particularly true with the Venezuelans, who were either in high spirits or quite depressed. So I tried alternating hill work, leg-speed work, and long-distance running. They not only got results, but also psychological advantages that fully justified the change. This regimen can initially hurt the legs quite severely, so study your reactions and remember that it is better to go easy in this phase than to overdo it. Feel your way into a pattern that suits you. Only well-conditioned athletes will get through the six weeks properly and successfully.

I should mention here that in all the years I have trained athletes on this hill program I have not had one develop achilles tendon trouble, an injury quite prevalent in sport today. Athletes are always running into hamstring and tendon trouble because they haven't done enough suppling and stretching exercises, or hill work to build resistance and to extend important muscles and tendons.

In a six-week period, there is an almost total renewal of red cells in your body. Since this coincides with the length of the initial anaerobic training, there will be a significant change in your general metabolism.

Your mileage during this period will be about 150 kilometers a week, including warming up and cooling down. Try to fit in other easy running each day to supplement this, since light aerobic exercise aids recovery. Ideally, you should aim for about 30 minutes of supplementary running each day.

For the leg-speed training, you need a flat area, 100 to 120 meters long, preferably with a slight gradual decline. Warm up for at least 15 minutes, and then run over the course up to ten times, thinking only about moving your legs as fast as possible. There should be a 3-minute interval between each run; it is important not to rush this exercise. Don't be conscious of stride length. Keep your upper body relaxed and the knee action reasonably high. You'll have the feeling your legs aren't moving fast enough. So run with a subconscious stride, thinking about pulling the legs through fast using the quadriceps and lower abdominal muscles. The exercise is designed to overcome stress in the legs and to develop fine speed. Avoid running into the wind as resistance is not desired. After the last repetition, cool down for at least 15 minutes, jogging easily.

This exercise will give you tired legs, but if you keep at it, it will become progressively easier after about two weeks. By then, you should be getting excellent results. So there it is: hill training three days a week, leg-speed running on the alternate days, and a long aerobic run on the seventh day.

Chapter 4

Track Training

I've often watched runners training, and then asked them what they were doing, what effect training was having on their bodies, why they were doing it, and what they hoped to achieve from it. Mostly, they didn't know. They were training blindly, guessing and hoping for good results. Some were slavishly following schedules that some champion had previously used, but they didn't understand the schedules or the general effects of the programs. Many had never asked their coaches why they were doing the particular work set for them. An athlete should know why a certain exercise is being used and how it will affect him.

Even if you're well conditioned, you will not have success if you don't evaluate your exercises and get a balance in your schedule. It's easy to make mistakes in track training and they can be disastrous. You could run your best races at unimportant meetings, come to the big ones off-peak, level off your performance too soon, or never reach your potential at all.

Many coaches and athletes overvalue track training and schedules, not realizing the most important training involves conditioning the body to prepare it for anaerobic training and racing. Without that preparation, track schedules are not worth the paper they are written on. The same is true of the track schedules included in this book, as guides to athletes and coaches preparing their own. If you don't condition first, they're useless.

When you move into track training, you must evaluate all the available types of running training. You must balance your schedule to get the best possible results from the conditioning work you've already completed. The tempo of training should be increased gradually and your speed controlled if you want to achieve the ultimate racing form when you need it. As in the previous phases of training, patience is imperative.

You will need increased volumes and intensities of anaerobic training, as well as sprint training, fast relaxed running, and sprint racing to help speed development. You'll need sharpening training to bring you to racing form; time trials to coordinate stamina and speed; racing in sprint, middle-, and long-distance races for improving racing condition; and experience to coordinate all of these.

DEVELOPING SPEED

Your original plan was to develop sufficient stamina to maintain the necessary speed over the distance of the race for which you are training. By now you should have developed fine endurance. With the initial resistance and anaerobic work finished, you should be ready for further development of your speed and anaerobic capacity to exercise, and sharpening and coordination of speed and endurance. At this stage your speed has not yet been fully developed. That has not been the prime objective of your training so far. Now it becomes of prime importance: it's the target of the next phase of training, with its more intense anaerobic activity.

Many athletes make the mistake of running in hard races before fully developing their speed. They find themselves unable to keep up with other athletes, although they finish feeling as if they could run the race all over again. Their inability to get speed into their running is frustrating.

Intense anaerobic training will not necessarily develop speed, since the volume of work involved and the increase in lactic acid preclude using top speeds. But workouts will develop your ability to exercise anaerobically. One of the best ways is to do fast, relaxed speed running for 100 to 150 meters, with recovery intervals of at least 3 minutes between each run so you can develop the same top speed again and again.

The fundamentals of building speed have to be watched carefully. In addition to fast, relaxed speed running, the sprint training workout should incorporate three elements emphasized by Bud Winter, former sprint coach at San Jose State University. These include some high-knee exercise running, some ankle flex and driving running, and some running-tall. For example, a typical workout, depending on your age and other factors, could be: proper warm-up, some suppling and loosening exercises, and a run of 80 to 100 meters with shoulders and arms relaxed, on the toes, pulling the knees up high, and using fast leg action with slow forward momentum. Take a 3-minute jog or walk and then run through it again—always working with the wind behind you so that there's no unnatural resistance.

Repeat once more, this time bringing the knees well up, but driving hard forward so that the ankles are flexed hard like a spring to force you forward. This should also be done twice, with a 3-minute recovery. Then twice, run down the track, high on your toes, with good knee-lift, concentrating on lifting your body from the pelvis. Percy Cerutty, the Australian distance coach, and Bud Winter have both recommended this. It's a good method for making the most of stride length, putting spring into the stride, and improving body lift.

Then make two faster runs over the course, running-tall but concentrating on all three aspects—stride length, spring, and body lift. You should also concentrate on these in the following fast running.

Following these exercise runs, use the straight of the track with a following wind, if any. Stride fast and relaxed the length of the straight, and then jog easily around the rest of the circuit before again running fast and relaxed down the straight. This can be done six or eight times according to your development and fitness. Then cool down by jogging for about 15 minutes or more.

Initially, track training, other than sprint training, should not be at full speed. Rather, the tempo should be held back a little so that it can be raised as you progress. Speed should always be controlled, or you'll lose control of racing form later.

When the schedule is arranged and the various runs are timed, pay attention to your capabilities and present condition. Allow reasonable times for each training run. Later on, you should run in previously determined times, but not faster. As always, you must have a clear picture in your mind of what you are doing, why, and what the short- and long-term effects will be.

Training should never be raced—a mistake many runners make. Such runners sharpen to racing condition before they reach the best coordination of stamina and speed, and as a result don't get the best possible results. It's not easy for a well-conditioned runner to refrain from gauging his speed during early training sessions; but this is necessary and important. Some coaches are often eager, early in the track training period, to see what their charges can do, and run the fine edge right off them.

If careful speed control is maintained, ten weeks of track training before the important competition should not be too long. A well-conditioned runner will show good results on less than this, but better results are possible if more time is taken, with a slower rise in tempo and rigid control of speed.

The schedules in this book have been used successfully in various international competitions and are responsible for several world records. So they are a reasonable guide to athletes and coaches. But they are only a guide. Don't stick strictly to them. All athletes have individual strengths and weaknesses, and these aspects merit careful consideration in shaping suitable schedules.

TRAINING EXERCISES

You need knowledge of exercise evaluation if you want to use suitable daily exercises for the best coordinated effort. So study the exercises carefully as they appear in the schedules.

The main types of training we will be concerned with are:

1. *Fartlek.* Swedish for "speed-play." This involves running at various speeds over forest trails, parks, and the countryside at will. It is invaluable throughout training because it allows for subconscious control of effort. It incorporates aerobic and anaerobic running, usually according to the condition and capabilities of the runner. Easy fartlek running is ideal for assisting in recovery from hard training and racing. Hard fartlek training can be used to develop anaerobic capacity.

2. *Paarlauf training.* This can be used for anaerobic training, speed development, and sharpening. It will depend on the number of runners taking part, the distances run, and the length of each session. It has value in that an athlete often subconsciously uses extra effort because of the competitive nature of the training. This is a form of relay racing, using predetermined distances around the track with an overlap of one runner. Runners continue to race other teams until stopped by a signal at a predetermined time, say, 4 minutes.

3. *Time trials.* If you give your body a certain exercise to do

often enough, you will become efficient at it. The same can be said about running over certain distances. The idea is to run trials under or near the distance you are training for. For 800 meters, for instance, you should run 600- and 700-meter trials; for 1,500 meters, you should run 1,000- and 2,000-meter trials. For these two events it is usually best to use some under-distance trials because of the high speeds involved and the resulting oxygen debts. For 3,000 and 5,000 meters, time trials can be at the same distances, but for 10,000 meters use mostly 5,000 meters with an occasional 10,000.

Steeplechasers should run trials over the actual distance, but on most trials it would be wise to do another hurdle instead of the water-jump. The effort used should be near to racing effort without increasing the speed over the final stage. Strong, even running is the best approach.

Time trials are most important in bringing about coordination of speed and stamina. They also help determine weaknesses and strengths, which indicate what further training and racing is needed to improve the former and capitalize on the latter.

4. *Starting practice.* For middle-distance runners, this exercise helps improve reflexes and sharpens and coordinates body actions, particularly when the intervals between starts are varied. The starts can be over distances of 30, 40, and 50 meters.

5. *Repetitions.* These are usually used for the development of anaerobic capacity by varying the numbers run, the distance, the time each run takes, and the intervals. Where control of the intervals is considered important, this is also called interval training. It is optional whether you select this or other anaerobic training to develop anaerobic capacity.

You should understand what you are trying to achieve with anaerobic training and work accordingly. In this system of repetitions, you run until the oxygen debt incurred makes you feel tired, indicating that you have developed a low blood pH. The times of the repetitions and intervals, the number of repetitions, and the distances run are not really important. If you have pulled your blood pH down at the end of the session, you have achieved what you set out to do. You are usually the best judge of when you have had enough, so the numbers of repetitions given in the schedules should be used only as general guidelines. They should be suited to your own needs.

6. *Sharpeners.* These are introduced when it is still necessary to do some anaerobic training, but it is advisable to drop the volume and increase the intensity. If you run 400 meters twenty times, you'll be at it for a long time and you'll become very tired. But if you run five laps of the track by sprinting 50 meters in every 100 meters, floating the other 50 (twenty sprints in all), you'll be extremely tired, but it will take only about 7 minutes. This sharpening puts the knife-edge on anaerobic training capacity, and brings you into racing shape without pulling down the good condition you have carefully built up. It's best to use this training only once a week, say on a Monday.

7. *Sprint training.* This is used purely for the development of speed. You should train with concentration on upright body carriage, a relaxed upper body, good knee-lift, and use of the ankles for driving. Allow good recovery intervals between fast runs.

The first four weeks of track training, you should work to get anaerobic capacity as high as possible, while concentrating on speed work until sprinting ability is near maximum. These types of training should be alternated day by day to allow for recovery from the harder anaerobic running. If you feel that recovery from anaerobic training is not sufficient, it's unwise to do more until the blood pH is near normal again. You should supplement this training with as much aerobic running as possible. This helps recovery from anaerobic running and keeps the oxygen uptake level high.

This is exacting, tiring training, so it is unwise to try to race, since it will be impossible for you to give good performances. Just concentrate on these two developments—anaerobic capacity and speed—with two or three days of anaerobic training, two or three of speed or sprint training, and other days of jogging, easy striding for technique, or easy fartlek. Your daily training should depend on your reactions to previous training. The training tempo should build gradually, with increased efforts as the days go by.

Track training should continue for about four and a half weeks to coordinate the training you've done so far. With your anaerobic capacity, speed, and stamina more or less developed, you now should aim to run smoothly through your competitions without apparent weaknesses showing in your running. You might have fine speed, stamina, and anaerobic capacity, but this doesn't necessarily mean you can race to your best potential. This is why time trials and development racing are needed. Development races are run while you are still training quite hard; you can't continue that and expect to run your best races at the same time. This is a mistake runners make the world over.

Sharpeners should be used at least once a week to maintain the anaerobic level. Pay attention to maintenance of speed as well. You should run at least one sprint race a week, on the same day as the less important competition or time trial training session. One day should be used for a longish aerobic run to help recovery; easy fartlek running can also help. Easy striding and jogging on the days before the hardest weekly race will be beneficial.

A schedule for this period could be: Monday, sharpeners; Tuesday, sprint training or easy fartlek; Wednesday, race, time trial, sprints, and middle distance; Thursday, use for coordinating, according to the results of the time trials or races (pace-judgment runs, fartlek, sharpeners, sprint training, or striding); Friday, jogging or easy stride-outs; Saturday, race over or near your racing distance or time trial; Sunday, a long, easy run.

FINAL TRAINING PERIOD

The last time trial should be run about ten days before the first important competition for which you're training. It should be run at your best effort. During the last one and a half weeks before that race, you should try to freshen up by lightening the training to build your mental and physical reserves. Some have called this "super compensation." It is important, however, and the period of time you need for this should be decided through trial and error methods in less important competitions. Individuals differ in the time they need, although about ten days suits most athletes. You should train every day during this period, but well within your capabilities. If you use fast running, it should be short and intense, not prolonged. The longer runs should be made at an easy pace.

Watch your food intake during this time. There can be a tendency to ease up in training and overeat. It is not desirable to put on any weight. So if you are susceptible to weight gain, take particular care.

When you reach the main competitions, it is important to realize that you are trained to race. So you need not train hard any longer. Again, this is a mistake made by many athletes. You need to keep fresh and sharp to race well; you can't do this if you try to train hard and race at the same time. A typical week's schedule for this period would be: Saturday, race; Sunday, an easy, longish run; Monday, a few sharpeners or easy fartlek; Tuesday, light sprint training session or stride-outs; Wednesday, race sprints and middle- or short-distance; Thursday, jog; Friday, stride-outs; and so on.

It is important to race or have time trials at least twice a week once racing begins. You should also observe the reactions of the previous day's exercise when deciding what to do each day.

Every day, do some supplementary long aerobic running, either in morning jogs or in good cooling-down runs after racing or training. This helps to maintain good condition, while aiding recovery from fast running. Observe how your legs feel after fast training and racing. If they feel dead, with no bounce, don't do anaerobic training in any volume; it's wiser to jog easily.

During the later stages of track training, it isn't possible to be too specific, as runners have different strengths and weaknesses and react differently to the coordinating training. Therefore, it's important to carefully analyze the training results of development races and time trials, and aim your training at repairing any apparent weaknesses. This is basically the way to approach track training for middle- and long-distance running. As long as the daily exercises are evaluated and you are confident the training you are doing is what you need, you will gain a fine balance in your schedule and achieve the desired results. Even if you train hard for long periods, your potential will not develop unless you train systematically and intelligently.

Chapter 5

Cross-Country Training

PHYSICAL BENEFITS

Cross-country running is of great benefit to track runners and other athletes as a general conditioner. Since the ground you run over is usually uneven and undulating, leg muscles and tendons are subjected to various resistances not encountered on even surfaces. They are often stretched to greater extremes, adding extra suppleness and strength. For instance, on soft ground your heels and toes sink deeper, giving the ankles greater range of movement, eventually improving flexibility. Ankle strength and flexibility are important developments in running; cross-country running is one of the best ways of helping these developments.

Athletes who run with stiff or taut upper body muscles or use an exaggerated leg-driving action can develop more relaxed and economical running techniques by training and racing cross-country. We've already explained that relaxed running is vital if you want optimum results from your racing. If you're not too relaxed, get out on muddy, sandy, or soft ground where it is difficult to gain good footing and traction. You'll soon learn that driving hard on these surfaces consumes energy rapidly and is extremely tiring. You'll also learn that the solution is to relax the upper body muscles, keep the arm action low, hold the hips forward, and develop a pulling action rather than a driving one. The effort of forward movement will be reduced to a minimum.

Poorly conditioned runners are inclined to run with tight upper body muscles and high arm carriage. The more tired they get, the worse these faults become and the more inefficient their running. So it makes good sense to get rid of these faults in your own run-

51

ning by working out on terrain that forces you to relax and economize.

The hilly terrains of cross-country courses have another value. Hill running offers resistance, adding a further dimension to the encouragement of ankle flexibility. Running uphill develops power and ankle suppleness, which later induce a more driving, natural stride. The steeper the hills, the more the ankle and leg muscles will have to flex.

Heavy runners will find this uphill running much more difficult. But leg muscle resistance will give added speed, power, and muscular endurance no matter what your shape and weight and how much you are forced to struggle. The greater the body weight, the more energy is needed to lift the body against gravity.

Running up hills forces you to lift the knees higher. This is one of the most desirable developments for any runner, as this governs stride speed and length. It also develops the muscle fibers, thus increasing power. Both red and white muscle fibers improve in efficiency with hill training.

Though lightweights usually beat heavyweights over hilly cross-country and track steeplechase courses, this shouldn't discourage heavily built runners. Everyone can gain vastly from cross-country work. I have invariably found that the runners who don't like cross-country running are the ones who need it most and find it most difficult to handle. The cause is usually poor and uneconomical technique. Such individuals are the ones who must persevere to overcome their faults.

PSYCHOLOGICAL VALUE

There is a psychological value to training over country, on forest trails, or around golf courses and parks. You'll find that you'll run over these terrains in a nonpressured way, speeding up or slowing down according to the lay of the land, the conditions, and your personal reactions. Accurate timing is impossible, so you tend to run at speeds that make you pleasantly tired rather than exhausted. This pace is often near your best aerobic speed, but you achieve it in a relaxed frame of mind. Runners seldom train over country at sustained anaerobic speeds unless they're carrying out some form of fartlek training—and that type of training is only employed in more advanced stages of physical fitness.

Racing cross-country is also psychologically good for you. These races don't have the same nervous tensions as track and road races, where the athlete is continually under the critical eyes and urgings of the spectators. There isn't the sustained speed running, so the overload tends to be on the muscular system, easing pressure on the cardiac system. This reduces the oxygen debt and allows for reasonable, rather than excessive, states of fatigue. There is no question that the presence of spectators influences tired runners to strive to maintain uneconomic speeds. Over country, your audience loses sight of you and there's no loss of face if you slow your speed to counter tiredness. Your running is generally much more relaxed.

Despite this, cross-country is good discipline. You will subconsciously control your effort to be more economical, which initially makes it a good general conditioning exercise. Later, it becomes important for runners to maintain controlled pressure on themselves over measured courses to ensure further development. But, initially, this isn't needed, and cross-country running helps you to avoid it.

CROSS-COUNTRY TECHNIQUE

During cross-country racing and training, don't concentrate on timing your runs. Courses and weather conditions will vary from day to day and considerably affect performance. Paying too much attention to progressive times can be confusing and misleading, so you should aim only to keep to an estimated effort schedule.

Cross-country will emphasize the value of calisthenics and suppling and stretching exercises. These help in handling fences, hurdles, and other obstacles encountered during racing and training. In fact, you should practice hurdling and clearing fences regularly, so that you achieve confidence and efficiency. The first time you encounter them, fences and hurdles can look forbidding. But with practice, they become more of an interesting challenge to your technique.

Before you race over an unfamiliar course, jog or walk over it and try clearing the various obstacles, practicing each until you feel confident and have worked out the best approach to clear it. Gymnastic ability is a distinct advantage in cross-country competition. You may need to use one- or two-handed vaults, depending on the height of the fences and the ground conditions leading up to them. It's also advisable to practice rolling under wire fences. It may be a messy method but it's often faster and easier than climbing them. Jumping, vaulting, hurdling, and rolling are all necessary arts.

If you intend to train seriously for cross-country events, as well as use cross-country for conditioning, you need to work out a schedule for the ten weeks preceding the race you're aiming for. This schedule, which is outlined later, is a mixture of anaerobic running (including sharpeners and longer repetitions), time trials, and races around the distance for which you're training. Before you begin this schedule, you need two or three months of aerobic cross-country running, especially if you have been competing on the track. If you're in poor condition, the aerobic conditioning period should be longer.

In some countries, cross-country races are no better than glorified track races. This is particularly so in many of the American states, where cross-country races are run on flat lawnlike areas. This isn't cross-country, since on such courses you run almost as you would on the road. This involves fast, sustained speed running, which doesn't help to condition because the exercise becomes sustained and anaerobic, encouraging cardiac fatigue. Such courses often don't even have obstacles. Athletes who compete on this type of course consistently once or twice a week for ten weeks invariably worsen their condition, rather than build it up. It's the rugged courses that really give you the benefits you want.

Back in 1950, when I left the Lynndale club in Auckland and joined Owairaka, I was faced with an interesting challenge. Lynndale was then the strongest cross-country club in New Zealand and Owairaka was barely developed. I began with six runners and in four years Owairaka was the top club in the country. It still is. One of the main reasons was that the young people in the Owairaka area, although they just came along to run, were trained and conditioned on one of the most rugged cross-country courses anywhere. Halberg, Puckett, Julian, Snell, and all my other runners were trained extensively on this course.

So, whether you're an athlete or a coach, you should consider cross-country as an important facet of preparation for track racing. You will encounter good obstacles, hills, muddy ground, and some flat fast running—a real mixture that tests runners in several ways. It slows them down through muscular fatigue as they hit the resistance of the hills, but allows them to speed up on the flat sections.

The runner gains suppleness by training for the obstacles, and learns to relax by jumping small streams and bogs and covering soft ground. For sprinters, middle- and long-distance runners, it's a great developer. And it would probably help athletes to condition for a number of other sports as well.

Track athletes should look on the cross-country season as an opportunity to build up general condition and to race as often as advisable. While concentrating on a relaxed running action, you will enjoy the environment in which you are exercising, whether it's woods, parkland, or rough pasture. It will make a surprising contribution to your development—physically, mentally, and in running technique.

Chapter 6

Racing Tactics

Middle- and long-distance racing is governed by eleven elements, all of which can be considered tactical. These include:

1. the athlete's basic abilities and development
2. basic speed or the ability to sprint
3. endurance
4. the ability to maintain a fast, steady pace
5. the ability to vary speed in a race
6. the most suitable distance for a finishing kick
7. the ability to exercise control during a race
8. consideration of opposing runners' abilities
9. the ability to observe and assess the weaknesses and strengths of the opposition
10. the ability to relate one's weaknesses and strengths to that of the opposition
11. the ability to judge pace

USE OF BASIC SPEED

You must always be realistic and understand your limitations in running various distances. It is important to consider all the above principles—particularly that of basic speed. Some runners are at a disadvantage because they don't have good basic speed, and must force the pace in most races. They fear the final fast kicks of their opponents, and must work hard to take that kick out of them. Very often this can be achieved; but there are exceptions. For instance, if there is a strong wind, fast runners can sit in on the man forcing the pace, letting the wind take its toll, and setting up a situation for a sprint finish when he is tired out. In such a situation, it is unwise for one to force the pace nearly all the way. It is better to sprint about 500 meters from the finish, which is far enough to test the opposition's stamina and weaken them for the final sprint. If you're trying this tactic, however, beware that you don't run out of energy yourself. It is best to try yourself out over various distances to determine the most suitable distance from the finish to begin your finishing run.

Some runners can pick up speed quickly; others have to build up to sprinting speed gradually. If you can kick fast, it is all right to be near the front when you kick. If you can't, you would be wise to stay back a few meters to give yourself some distance to gather speed before passing the leaders. Otherwise, you'll take them with you; you won't be able to shake them off and will not gain any advantage from being the one who breaks first. This is a situation in which you need to know your opposition: anyone in that field, behind you or in front, could produce a faster kick and pass you before you've built up your own sprint. Again, trial and error methods will show you the most suitable kicking distance.

Runners with questionable stamina have been known to try slowing the pace by taking the lead and gradually slowing the speed. This works at times, but in most races, other runners soon realize what is happening and pass the leader to pick up the speed again. Then, the runner trying to ease the pace back must once again try to lead. Invariably, this results in a series of sprints that take toll of the runner lacking stamina, reducing, rather than enhancing, his possibilities.

Usually, it is better for a runner with questionable stamina to keep on the inside track line, covering as little ground as possible, and hoping that the speed will not be too fast, so he can use his own speed near the end. Trailing the front-runner is more likely to help control the pace than front-running. Front-runners often have doubts flitting through their minds about whether they can maintain the speed; these doubts build up nervous tensions that can tie them up. When the dreaded—and by now expected—sprint burst comes from another runner, front-runners often lack a reply and let the rest of the field go by. Very few important international races are won from the front. This confirms that it is wise to stay back if the speed is reasonable, and avoid making your run too soon. Few athletes can muster two sprints of more than 100 meters in the same race. So it is best to conserve your energy, both mentally and physically, for that one concerted burst for the tape when you can afford to hold nothing back.

Twenty years ago, when most distance runners lacked the endurance of the top runners of today, it was possible for a runner like Russia's Kutz to put in a series of wind sprints of about 50 meters during a 5,000-meter race, and leave the opposition gasping for breath. You can no longer be sure of this tactic, however. Some runners may fall off the pace if subjected to a series of sprints, but the majority are likely to absorb them as well as the runner applying them.

TIMING THE SPURTS

To run well, tactically, requires fine control and pace judgment. Too often, runners go off too fast for their ability, simply because someone else has done so and they are foolish enough to follow. They get themselves into a large oxygen debt too early and find themselves paying the price near the end of the race.

Of course, if the runner has plenty of stamina, and must use his endurance to win, it is sometimes worth the gamble to make the early pace fast. But the wind must not be too strong, and the runner hopes that faster runners will be foolish enough to follow. If he is matched against experienced runners, it is unlikely they will follow. In this situation it is sometimes possible to take a breather and then speed up again.

Study the likely opposition as much as you can, both locally and in other areas. Find out everything you can about their individual strengths and weaknesses. You should even take notes for future reference. You may read about runners from other countries and discount them; but you never know when you are going to find yourself in the same race with one of them. If you've then forgotten what you read, you could be penalizing yourself, either by failing to exploit weaknesses or by playing into the opposition's hands by running their kind of race. You must aim to run the race in a way that causes your opponents the utmost problems.

Always remember that the shortest way to the finish is on the inside track, and that every time you get away from it you are running farther than the actual distance of the race. The wise runner keeps as close to the inside as possible, and only moves out to pass other runners or to position himself on the track for his final kick.

In many 800-meter races, runners cover the first 300 meters in lanes. The runners in the outer lanes then often leave their lanes and cut nearly straight toward the inside, losing 6 or more meters. If they aimed for the far inside corner and headed directly for that, they would save themselves valuable meters of running they will need at the end of the race.

Runners who suddenly put in bursts from positions in the middle of the field, take up another trailing position, and then drift back through the field again are wasting their efforts. If you intend to make a move in a race, put some purpose into it and, having achieved your goal, don't let it go again.

TACTICAL MISTAKES

There are countless races in which athletes should have run better races, but didn't because of tactical mistakes or unintelligent running. Dave Bedford's 1971 European 10,000-meter championship race in Helsinki was one of them. Before the race, he was tested for fitness by Swedish physiologists and said to have an oxygen uptake of 87 milliliters per kilogram, one of the highest recorded. This led to statements that Bedford was more or less unbeatable. But people didn't take into account other factors, like tactics.

Bedford was a front-runner, used to running his opposition into the ground, getting clear about halfway, and continuing on to victory unchallenged. Unfortunately for him, in this race there were other runners who had prepared well and could now match his speed in the first 5,000 meters and stay close to him throughout. Bedford is also not the most economical runner. When he found himself in front but not clear of the field, it was apparent that he began to tie up with nervous tension. At the bell, several runners sprinted past him. They finished with a 53-second final lap, leaving him floundering in their wake. The winner, Vaatainen of Finland, didn't run nearly as fast as Bedford's best performance, but, tactically, he was the master of the day. I believe that if Bedford had not tried to run this fine field into the ground early, but had settled into a strong, steady pace, using the last 5,000 meters to apply pressure, he would have fared better and would certainly not have tensed up as he did. Bedford's world record for 10,000 meters still stands as proof of his undoubted ability, but it is significant that

Dave Bedford leading in a 10,000-meter race between Great Britain and West Germany in London, 1971. (Photograph by Tony Duffy.)

he didn't usually run like that in important competitions.

PLANNING THE STRATEGY

The 1964 Tokyo Olympic steeplechase, won by Belgium's Gaston Roelants, was one of the finest tactical races I have ever witnessed. Roelants was noted for starting fast in his races and running the rest into the ground early, rather like Bedford, while maintaining his advantage to the end.

But in the semifinals, Roelants began to tire noticeably after 2,000 meters, and did not look as fit as he had previously. When the final field lined up two days later and the gun was fired, Roelants didn't go to the front as he usually did. It was apparent that the rest of the runners were confused by this; they seemed at a loss about what to do. So, instead of the pace being fast early, as it normally was with Roelants in the field, it was slow. Nobody was anxious to take over the lead, and everyone muddled along in confusion, reluctant to force the pace. But with 1,000 meters gone, Roelants suddenly jumped into the lead and began running as he usually did at the beginning of a race. He completely caught the others by surprise, gaining a good lead that he was able to hold until the finish.

It seemed to me that Roelants had realized that if he ran his usual front race, making it hard for everyone else, he would tire before the finish. But he calculated he could last out a fast 2,000 meters, and so planned his front race from there. His rivals had neither anticipated nor could counter his switch of tactics.

Murray Halberg's 5,000-meter win in the Rome Olympics in 1960 was an example of hard-way tactics. His plan was simply to jump the field with three laps to go and run himself out to stay in front. It was the only way, we reasoned, of making sure he would win it.

The theory for Halberg's tactic was based on something that impressed me in my early days of training. I found then in training for the 3 miles that, if I prepared over 6 miles and over 1 mile, it did not necessarily means that I would run a good 3 miles. I had to accustom myself to the actual speed required over 3 miles. Hence the use of time trials in my schedules. Most 3-milers belong to one of two types: the natural miler, or the 6-miler. The miler finds the early pace well within his compass, and in the nervous tension of a big race may be inclined to go fast too early. Consequently, between 1¾ and 2¼ miles he will begin to tire. The 6-miler, a stayer, finds the early speed difficult to cope with. About the time the miler is beginning to sag, the stayer begins to wonder if he can maintain that speed to the finish.

So, in most 3-mile and 5,000-meter races, there is, at this point, a general moment of indecision and reluctance. You can actually feel that indecision. The pace slackens and falters; no one, except a trained and alert 5,000-meter man, like Halberg was, is prepared to go. That is the psychological time to strike and that is why Halberg went. He'd already pulled the same break successfully in the Empire Games in Cardiff.

The last time I won the New Zealand marathon title in Auckland I used the weather tactically to upset my opposition. The prerace favorite, Richards, was from Christchurch, a much cooler town than Auckland. The day of the race was a typical Auckland one, with high humidity.

Richards had run 2:30 for the marathon, which was good running in 1955. But I reasoned that the Auckland heat would get to him if I encouraged it. I cracked on the pace for 3 or 4 miles, dragging the field after me, and then eased back out of it. The chance I took paid off. With 6 miles left, I was seventh, with Richards about a mile ahead. But since I was fresher than he was, I was able to run the last mile in five minutes, while he struggled over it in eight. I passed him, and covered the last lap to the finish before he started on it. Over the last few miles, the heat and humidity had completely beaten him down because the early speed had drained his reserves. If a runner is confident he is going to be difficult to beat, it pays to keep the information as secret as possible. Catch the opposition by surprise.

During the 1974 Commonwealth Games in Christchurch, I was advising Richard Tayler for his 10,000-meter race. His training had been interrupted by a pulled leg muscle, and he had lost some of his track training. But it was apparent, when he ran a 13:40 5,000-meter time trial with consummate ease ten days before the race, that he was going to be difficult to beat. The New Zealand press was trying to get all the news they could about the prospects of the runners; fortunately, David Bedford was getting the lion's share of the publicity. This suited us, because we were able to keep pressure off Richard. His best 10,000 meters was then only 28:24, but we knew he was in better form than ever before. As a

Richard Tayler and Frank Shorter at a 10,000-meter indoor meet in 1974. (Photograph by Jeff Johnson.)

runner who could run a 2:15 marathon and a sub-four-minute mile, he had both the speed and the stamina to win, provided he ran sensibly, kept an even pace, and stayed out of trouble.

I knew Bedford was a man who liked the front, so I guessed there would be a fair amount of jostling during the early stages of the race. I suggested that Tayler sit back while this happened, and move up only when the leaders had settled down, and some of them had dropped off the pace. I wasn't wrong. Both Bedford and the other English runner, Black, tried to keep up with the front-runners, and got several body checks that seemed to upset Bedford more than Black. I remarked to the English coach who was sitting with me that I wondered why he hadn't warned the two Englishmen to keep clear of the front-runners until they settled down. He admitted that he should have, as his runners were having a rough time.

At the halfway point, Tayler was about 60 meters behind the leaders, and looked as though he was out of contention. But once the leaders slowed down as the early pace took its toll, he gradually neared the four leaders and trailed. With two laps to go, Black took off. But he had little chance with Tayler, who not only had better speed but fine endurance. Tayler won comfortably by a good 60 meters, after a sustained sprint over the last 300 meters. His finishing time of 27:46 was a record for the race, and Tayler's best by about 40 seconds. Bedford had worked too hard early in the race and ruined any prospects he may have had.

Another race that was run nearly as planned was the 1965 Tokyo Olympic 1,500-meter final, in which I was fortunate to have two runners, Peter Snell and John Davies. I never discuss races on the day they are run, unless something unforeseen happens. I believe that athletes should be left to their own devices that day. Tensions can be introduced unnecessarily by talking about a race and trying to give advice in the final minutes. Peter, John, and I talked over our race tactics the night before. We felt that Snell's possibilities were great, but that John could not make a place if he got caught in a sprint finish, since his speed was not good enough. There were many faster men in the field.

John had tried a sprint finish in the semifinals from about 250 meters out, and had nearly given me heart failure because everyone else had the same idea and John was four lanes wide on the final bend, trying to outsprint faster men. He did manage to scramble

John Davies (467) leading Peter Snell (466), who went on to win the 1,500-meter final at the 1964 Tokyo Olympics. (Photograph by Mark Shearman.)

into fourth place—but just barely. We did not want this to happen again, so we decided that, with 800 meters to go, John would take over the pace and Peter would try to take up a place by his shoulder. Being a long-striding runner, he would be difficult to pass, and would force an overtaking runner to go out two or three lanes.

The man we considered a danger was the American, Dyrol Burleson, who had drawn the inside lane just inside John. So we planned that John would start off at the same pace as Burleson and keep him on the inside of the field. The Frenchman Michel Bernard was a front-runner, trained on interval training. Because of this, I did not think he would last three hard races, although I expected him to take the early lead.

It happened as though we had told all the runners beforehand what to do. Bernard took the lead. Burleson was inside Davies and the rest of the field. At 700 meters, Bernard began to flag and Davies quickly took over. But, before Snell could get up on the outside, another runner nabbed the place we had reserved for him. With 250 meters to go, Snell took off as planned. He had to get out of a boxed position to do this, but instead of dropping back and going round the field as he had done in the semifinal, he stuck out his right arm like a traffic signal and received an obliging gap from the Englishman, John Whetton. Davies sprinted as hard as he could. As they swept into the straight, the Englishman ran around Davies, forcing him to change course and slow a little. This let Josef Odlozil of Czechoslovakia pass, so that although Davies finished fast, he was nipped out of second, behind Snell, by a few centimeters. Burleson never did get out of the bunch. A few years later I overheard him remark, in discussing the race, "If I could have got out I would have won." I have often wondered if he knew how he got boxed in the first place. This was a successful tactical race because we knew the runners we were competing against, as well as the type of training they used. It was interesting, too, because, despite the calm with which Snell handled the last 400 meters, he actually ran them in 53.2 seconds, and the last 300 in 38.6 seconds.

There are times when you meet runners you know little or nothing about. If you meet them first in heats or semifinals, it pays to have your coach or another runner who is not competing look over the field and estimate their capabilities. This is usually necessary for athletes at Olympics because there you often compete with runners for the first time.

You can also test these runners out in heats or semifinals by running the race with a sharp finishing sprint to test their speed. You can make a longer sustained sprint as well, although the other runner won't always take the bait and sprint just when you hope he will. Usually, though, in the important competitions, once one runner starts to sprint, the others follow, unless the standard is poor. There are runners who continually mix the pace. This emphasizes the importance of pace judgment, so that you aren't fooled into an unnecessary series of wind sprints.

Pass other runners only in the straights unless there is no option but to pass on a bend. Keep to the pole line as much as possible; the further you stray from it, the longer the race becomes. Try to keep the pace as even and economical as possible. The runner who starts sprinting in the middle stages is unlikely to be sprinting at the end.

Go into every race with a plan in mind. Whether the race goes according to that plan will depend on many factors. But if you consider all possibilities and use logic, you will not be surprised by others' tactics and can quite often call the tune.

Since runners today are generally well conditioned and are trained to be prepared for any eventuality, the use of the various tactics is minimized. There will always be runners who try surprises; but current training means that, more and more, the main tactical weapon is the finishing sprint.

The 1956 Olympics was the last in which interval-trained athletes dominated middle- and long-distance running. With the dismal failure of the Germans in Melbourne, Dr. Gershler, who, with Dr. Riendell, was mainly responsible for the development and use of this training method, lost face with the German athletic authorities, coaches, and athletes.

In the next four years, Australian and New Zealand runners, training using marathon conditioning, eclipsed the efforts of athletes still using the older training methods. Elliott, Thomas, Power, and Lincoln from Australia, and Neville Scott and Halberg from my group, dominated international competitions between 1957 and 1959.

The 1960 Olympics proved the soundness of the Australasian technique, as Snell took the 800 meters, Elliott the 1,500, Halberg the 5,000, and Barry Magee ran third in the marathon, with the fastest time then recorded by a white man. This led to an international conference in West Germany to debate the merits of the system. A general switch in training by several countries followed.

The interval-trained runners opposing Halberg had trained to have rest periods. But Halberg's series of coordinating time trials had eliminated this weakness. Snell's strength was his ability to combine speed with better stamina than his opponents, even though he was a novice on the international scene. Magee was another novice; he'd run only two marathons before Rome. But he, Abebe Bikila, and the second medal-winner were all endurance-trained runners with highly developed oxygen uptake levels.

Rome was the most colorful Olympics I have attended. There was bright sunshine most days in a beautiful open-air stadium. There were no political problems and the crowds seemed to enter into the true spirit of the games. Tokyo was drab by comparison; it was usually overcast, rainy, and somewhat oppressive. There, Snell won the 800 and 1,500, while John Davies ran third in the 1,500. But Halberg was beaten by an attack of influenza the week of the games, and Neville Scott and Barry Magee had injuries. But Marise Chamberlain, running a magnificent race to take third in the women's 800 meters, and Bill Baillie made heroic attempts to redeem New Zealand's standing in distance running. There was some compensation when Billy Mills, of the USA, ran off with the 10,000-meter gold medal: he, too, had been trained with my marathon-type methods, under the guidance of an old pupil of mine, Australian Pat Clohessy.

Chapter 7

Training Summary

When should you start training?

The sooner you start the better, provided you are a healthy individual and are not suffering from any injury or ailment. Inactivity does not improve the efficiency of the body. The body's fitness does not stay at a given level, but either improves or deteriorates. If you do not exercise, you will not be as fit tomorrow as you are today.

Can training harm you, either early or later on?

Provided you train within your own fitness level to the "pleasantly tired state," or aerobically, your condition will invariably continue to improve, with your metabolism generally functioning better. Extreme use of anaerobic or excessive speed training can be detrimental to your health, as the continued low blood pH can upset the functions of some metabolic actions in your body. If you maintain a good ratio of aerobic exercise in your overall weekly schedule, you will continue to gain in general cardiac efficiency. Aerobic exercise cannot adversely affect a healthy heart. To the contrary, it will make it bigger, stronger, and generally more efficient.

How often should you train?

The more regularly you train the better. Dr. Hartialla of Finland once said: "The day that you do not train will take you two more days' training to get you back to where you were." This may not be exactly true, but it is close to being right. You should exercise daily, even if it is only a short jog of 10 to 15 minutes, rather than doing tiring workouts with days of rest in between. For an athlete, every day's training is important for maintaining your fitness level.

With youngsters, there are psychological aspects to consider, since most youths don't want to be involved with only one sport or recreation. So, if you're advising the young, tell them to play at the training and take some rest days if they really want to. Invariably, if they have a schedule to train to, they will be conscientious enough to try to keep to it. But youngsters' training should never become a task that takes away the pleasure.

Should you train more than once a day?

If time allows, it is advisable to train two or three times a day, provided there is no imbalance between aerobic and anaerobic efforts. Once the necessary anaerobic session has been completed— if there is one in the phase of the schedule you are working on— any supplementary easy or aerobic training will further improve you. This helps develop general cardiac efficiency and assists in the recovery from the low blood pH that may have developed during anaerobic training. By stimulating blood circulation gently or aerobically, you will assist your metabolism to improve generally.

Other aspects, including the energy expended at work, must also be considered. However, even when you're physically or mentally tired, an easy jog in a park can work wonders in assisting in your recovery and regaining your feeling of well-being.

How long in time or distance should you run?

This is an individual consideration, governed not by age, but more by physical fitness. Quite young runners can go for up to two hours or more without resting. It is usually best to try to run for a given time rather than a given distance, so you avoid putting pressure on yourself to complete a course or finishing in a state of fatigue. By running for a given time, you will not try to see how far you can go; you'll be governed by your feelings as you run and will quite often hold back in the early stages to make sure you finish the time comfortably.

It is advisable to run daily for a time that you know you can manage well. Then occasionally—say, twice a week—add another 15 to 30 minutes. This way you will gradually build up your endurance without getting into a fatigued state before completing a course. You will also avoid biting off more than you can chew in any training session. It is the speed that will stop you, not the distance to be run. If you go slow enough, you'll be able to complete progressively longer runs with ease. So, go for distance, not speed.

Where should you train?

Changes of scenery and different environments can stimulate you to train more consistently and better, so it pays to alter your training venues and courses from time to time. All sorts of terrain should be used often, with concentration on the terrain you will race over in a particular season. For instance, during the cross-country season, most of the work should be in the country.

But when you're training for the track, it is often advisable to do all the training possible away from the track, such as repetitions, sprint training of some types, and technique training. It can freshen your approach to training and make you more interested in the training you have to do on the track, such as trials and training work that require timing. The new synthetic tracks can cause tired or sore legs if they are used too often, because of the rebound that occurs when you're running fast.

For conditioning training to increase oxygen uptake, it is better to choose terrain that offers good traction, so you can run at a high aerobic effort without tiring your leg muscles too quickly. This is why roads are often best for high-volume aerobic running. Soft, rough, or sandy ground tires the muscles, slowing you and reducing the circulatory system's pressure.

How much anaerobic training should you do?

An anaerobic training session should stop when you are tired enough from the oxygen debt incurred. Coaches cannot define this limit beforehand, and can only offer advice about what work load is reasonable. You, the runner, must decide the stopping point, whether your training includes repetitions, interval work, or fartlek.

In what weather conditions is it inadvisable to train?

You can train in extremes of temperature—from −30°F to 105°F or even higher. However, if the temperature is low, it is important that the humidity is also low; otherwise your lungs can ice up. In Finland, the humidity is usually about 20 percent or less during very low temperatures; so Finns can run comfortably for two hours.

If the temperature is very high, you need a reasonably high humidity level too, so that your skin will stay wet with perspiration and help to cool your blood. If the humidity is low, you can dehydrate quite quickly and be forced to stop training. Remember: in high temperature, the humidity should be high; in low temperature, the humidity should be low. In other combinations, training becomes difficult, impossible, or even dangerous.

Watch the wind in low temperatures; it can blister unprotected skin. If you train in cold climates you need good protective clothing. Some runners suffer from hyperventilation because the muscles of the lower rib-cage controlling breathing become too cold to operate properly. Aprons of flannel or wool can be used to keep these muscles warm.

For heavy rain, it is wise to have good waterproof covering to keep out the worst of the rain and maintain reasonable warmth. If your legs are inclined to get cold, protect them by rubbing them all over with olive oil. It helps to maintain warmth and improves circulation.

Back in 1960, the late Perry Cerutty was in New Zealand on a lecture tour. He remarked that only four runners had then broken 28 minutes for 6 miles, and that two of them were Australians and none were English or New Zealanders. His air of scorn angered me because I knew Halberg could do it. He was off training then, but I went to him and he agreed to do it. Three nights later, although it was cold and wet and Halberg was faced with a wet, soft grass track, he made the attempt. Murray had a hot bath and smothered himself in a liberal layer of olive oil. We then wrapped him up well and took him to the track. He turned on what I think was an unequalled grass track performance: the world's second-fastest 6 miles (27:52.2) and the third-fastest 10,000 meters (28:48). I am convinced the olive oil treatment had a tremendous bearing on his handling of the poor conditions.

How long should you rest between seasons?

It is wise to keep training when one competitive season ends, rather than to stop altogether. The training need not be too exacting. Light jogging for at least 15 minutes a day will help maintain your general condition and make it easier once you begin schedule training again. As I have mentioned, your performance level in the next competitive season is governed by your aerobic capacity; the more training you can do to improve this the better.

So in the period between the end of the cross-country or track season and the beginning of the anaerobic training for the next competitive season, get in all the mileage possible. Two weeks of light jogging can help to freshen you up mentally and physically, and will maintain and probably improve your general condition.

How many days a week should you rest and not train?

If you are fifteen years old or younger and feel that training every day is too tiring, you can rest one or two days a week. But it is better physiologically to train every day if you keep the sessions well within your ability.

Mature athletes should train every day, but some of the days can be rather light. If you train only six days a week, you can't hope to beat athletes who train every day. Anyone who loses fifty-two days' training a year isn't going to have optimum results.

How many days should you rest before competitions?

If the competitions are important ones, then it is best to find out through trial and error what periods of rest or easing up suit you best. Some athletes run better if they train lightly during the last ten days and do nothing the two days immediately before the competitions. Others find it better to keep going, jogging or running through some fast stride-outs on the morning of the race. Whatever you do, realize that training hard during the last days before competitions can only make your performance worse. But jogging lightly will usually keep your bowels in good order and help your metabolism because of the stimulation of aerobic exercise on the circulation.

What total amount of anaerobic training should be used?

The maximum anaerobic capacity of the runner needs to be developed for optimal results. This involves the capacity to incur an oxygen debt of 15 to 18 liters. I have shown that it is possible to develop this capacity in individuals with three to four weeks of intensive anaerobic training sessions every other day, with the other days used for recovery training. Before this, some anaerobic running is used for about four weeks, in the form of 50-meter sprints extending up to 200 meters in series of threes or fours, three or four times a day, three times a week. This is to cover the transition period from the slower aerobic training to the intensive anaerobic training.

The East Germans work on a period of about five weeks. However, if you engage in anaerobic training of an intensive nature three days a week for about four weeks, you'll be close to developing your anaerobic capacity to the maximum. Without the assistance of physiologists, you can usually tell by your feelings whether you are getting exhausted by the training. If you are, it is wise to ease up on fast volume anaerobic training, and use short, fast wind sprints over 50 or 100 meters, plus racing and easy fartlek sessions. You should be able to maintain that comfortably.

This is an important part of the training to control, and it's difficult to estimate the volume and intensity of work that is most successful, because of differing individual reactions. Go by your own reactions and adjust your training to suit them. But remember that a hard anaerobic session must be followed by a recovery period before another anaerobic session to avoid keeping the blood pH depressed.

Should you be timed in training?

It pays to time some, but not all, of your training. To develop good pace judgment, times should be called to you or a whistle blown every 100, 200, or 400 meters until you develop an ability to judge pace accurately. With practice, you can develop this to a very marked degree.

On the other hand, I believe that too much use of the watch during training can be detrimental because it places too much pressure on you to maintain exacting efforts on some days. It is much wiser to train according to how you feel. This applies particularly to anaerobic repetition and interval training, phases that many give too much emphasis. If you work to efforts that you feel happy about, you'll gain the desired results. For time trials and even-paced running it pays to use your watch. It's all a question of what training you're doing and how much control you need. Just don't become a prisoner of the watch.

What is the use of running time trials?

The words *time trials* often give a wrong impression of their use. Basically, they are used to develop coordination in running races over certain distances, and to find any weaknesses and use the appropriate training to strengthen them. Time trials should not be run at full effort, but with strong, even efforts, leaving you with some reserves.

Don't place too much emphasis on the time resulting from time trials. The effects of any irregularities in your running are the important factors. Analyzing the lap times and discovering why there are variances will give you information of some value. If you get too concerned about the elapsed time, you're liable to lose confidence in your potential. Remember that when you are doing time trials, you are still training hard, so good times cannot always be expected. You cannot train hard and perform well simultaneously.

Part II

Preparation and Fitness

Chapter 8

Injury Prevention and Cure

People who run aerobically on the balls of their feet, with their heels touching afterward, are more susceptible to foot troubles than those who land nearly flat-footed, touching the heels down first and rolling onto the balls of the feet and toes. This is because when running aerobically the forward momentum is such that the body's center of gravity takes longer to pass over the lead foot. More traction develops when landing on the balls of the feet than when rolling off the heels, resulting in a braking action that can cause blistering, damaged toenails, metatarsal damage, and shin splints. It is therefore advisable for runners with tighter tendons in their legs or who naturally run this way to train on grass or sandy areas to lessen the traction. This will help alleviate possible problems.

KNEE INJURIES

Knee trouble can arise during conditioning work if the upper front leg muscles and sinews are too tight and stressed. These quadriceps must be strengthened by uphill running or by doing squats or other stretching exercises.

Ill-fitting or worn shoes can be a source of knee and hip trouble. They place stress on different parts of the legs depending on their state of wear. You should check them every week. If you are running correctly, the main wear should be on the back outer side of the heel, the outside of the forepart, and slightly on the toes. This wear shows you're running with balance. Wear should be even on both shoes. If it is not, it could indicate you are running with tight arm or shoulder muscles, badly fitting shoes, or even a skel-

etal defect that makes you run lopsided. This isn't entirely dangerous, but it is another reason for keeping your shoes in good order.

ACHILLES TENDON INJURY

Achilles tendon trouble is usually caused during resistance work,
when you may be trying to build powerful muscles without doing
enough suppling and stretching exercises. The importance of full
extension of muscles and sinews must be appreciated. A man working with weights seldom attains full extension of his legs until he
goes out and sprints—and at that point he's just not ready for it.

HAMSTRING TROUBLE

Hamstring trouble is caused by leg-speed running with muscles
and sinews that are not stretched and conditioned equally. Often
the quadriceps are more powerful than the biceps. This is yet
another reason for using calisthenics for the full range of movement, and concentrating on the running exercises we have outlined. Pulled muscles are caused by a breakdown of the sheathing
around muscle fibers, and tearing of the fibers themselves. The
causes are usually poor warming-up or poor conditioning. It can
happen even if all these things are done properly because the stress
of using these muscles for long periods can cause the breakdown
of muscle tissue. Even athletes who take every precaution can experience this trouble under the most perfect conditions.

When it does happen, you can put your finger accurately on the
spot. There will be bleeding there and you must stop it. Ice or cold
water are most effective. Treat it this way for three days before
you begin massage. By then scar tissue should form around the
affected area. Massage then helps to get rid of the excess blood
around the tissue, and to stimulate nutrients to the injured area.

In all cases of injury, go to a qualified physician rather than
treat yourself. You could make the damage worse. Even with
stresses of the knee and ankle joints, see a physician.

SHIN SPLINTS

Shin splints are membrane ruptures between the muscle and the
bone, and often arise because of the jarring of downhill running or
overstriding. You can counter overstriding by building up the front
of your shoes a little. You should always be cautious when running
downhill. Water therapy, cold packs, and heat treatment can help

to treat shin splints. Water therapy is invaluable for leg injuries generally. Even shin splints, which tend to be the most difficult to overcome, will respond. Just get into a tepid pool with a kickboard —and kick.

Injuries to joints and bone wear are invariably caused by poor buffers and jarring on hard surfaces. Without plenty of reasonably soft rubber between you and the ground, the shock of each stride is felt over a wide area of the body. Problems arise in unexpected places. You need padding that gives you a recoil from the ground. Shoes that achieve this are not cheap. But in the long run, you will save, because the damage you can suffer is difficult to eliminate, particularly in large persons. Consider the possible loss of training and competition time—and get good shoes.

All this advice gets back to one thing—it is better to prevent than it is to cure. Consider at the outset what you are going to do in your sport. Try to understand the stresses and estimate the weaknesses you may have to contend with. Then work to alleviate the problems in advance. Cushion yourself against shock and injury from the beginning.

Chapter 9

Warming Up, Warming Down

An American coach from Abilene College told me that he flew to Sacramento a few years ago to hear a lecture by Percy Cerutty. In the question and answer period, Percy was asked if it was necessary to warm up. "What do you want to warm up for?" Percy asked. "Rabbits don't and they can run like the very devil."

Knowing Percy as I do, I realize he was only saying this to make people think, but the Abilene coach and others took him seriously since he was then the greatest coach in the world.

The Abilene coach couldn't get home fast enough to find out if what Percy said about rabbits was true. He knew he could find a warren and he wanted to see for himself. He went out before daybreak with a movie camera and finally filmed a rabbit, which emerged from its burrow, sat on its hind legs, looked around, and trotted back and forth several times before suddenly taking off across the field. So, said the Abilene coach, rabbits *do* warm up and I've got a film to prove it. Percy had succeeded in making him think, question, and find the answers.

THE REASON FOR WARM-UPS

When runners warm up for middle- and long-distance races, you'll notice there is a big difference in the time they take. There are various factors that influence athletes' warm-ups, but it is most important to understand why you need to warm up at all. The main reasons are: (1) to raise blood circulation to a pulse rate near 130 to 140 beats a minute, so that you don't have to "go through the gears" in your race; and (2) to raise the body temperature and loosen up the muscles so they can function more efficiently, re-

85

ducing the risk of pulling a muscle or straining a tendon. The warm-up overcomes muscle sluggishness and sets you free to run easily at your best effort.

Years ago, athletes didn't bother with the warm-up, and early in a middle- or long-distance race would hope to get a "second wind." You can now achieve this in the warm-up by raising the blood circulation. It's best to get through this difficult and possibly risky period before you begin racing. In the race, you're under the strain of running competitively and unable to control your effort without risking your position in the field.

When a muscle is cold, it is tight and less efficient than when it is warm. Warmth brings softness and reduces tightness, allowing faster contractions.

The kind of warm-ups you do depends on the type of competition. The steeplechase, for instance, calls for some calisthenics to prepare you for the hurdling involved. It's also a question of preference. Some runners ignore calisthenics and confine their warm-ups to running at various speeds. Others, particularly those who incorporate calisthenics in their training programs, like to include them as part of the warm-up process. As long as you understand what you're trying to achieve and use exercises to achieve your goal, it isn't too important how you go about it.

LENGTH OF WARM-UPS

Time your warm-up according to the conditions of the particular day. If it's windy and cold, it will naturally take you longer to warm up, even if you wear warmer clothing. But don't forget that, hot or cold, the pulse rate will begin rising as soon as you start running. Many athletes take far too long for their warm-ups. Some warm up for thirty to forty-five minutes or longer on days with moderate temperatures and reasonably good conditions. But they could lift their pulse rates and body temperatures to the required levels in fifteen minutes or less. They get involved in long warm-ups usually because they don't really understand *why* they are doing it.

I recall arriving at the venue of the Finnish marathon championship in 1968, about an hour before the start, and seeing some of the runners already engaged in their warm-ups. I mentioned to a companion that these runners did not understand what they were doing. Some of them were running even faster than they would be halfway through the race. And that's actually what happened.

A marathon doesn't really require much warm-up at all. As long as pulse rate and body temperature are a little higher than normal, you'll be fine, because the initial pace is never as fast as it is in a track race. Those who do go off like Cerutty's startled rabbits invariably drop back after a few kilometers.

Fifteen minutes is long enough for middle- and long-distance racing. You should begin with seven or eight minutes at a good aerobic speed, follow with some 50- to 100-meter wind sprints according to how you feel—about three is usually enough—and then jog easily to keep up your pulse and body warmth. Just before the race, discard your track suit, but keep moving about easily until you are called to the mark. Don't make the mistake of runners who warm up adequately and then lie under a blanket for five minutes or more. They stay warm but their pulse rates fall, which nullifies the advantage they gain in the warm-up.

The runner who warms up for long periods gains nothing more physiologically than one who confines himself to 15 minutes. This is only recommended if he is of a nervous nature, and is more at ease trotting around than sitting down thinking about the race and adding to the tensions. Psychologically, as well, it might be of value for such a runner to keep moving. If he has a solid background of endurance training it won't do any harm, except perhaps in marathon or cross-country racing, when it is important to conserve all the energy possible.

WARMING DOWN

When you finish your race, it is also important to warm down or cool down. During the race your pulse rate is high, with blood gushing through the circulatory and respiratory systems under great pressure from the heart. When you stop and the pressure from the heart diminishes, many of the lesser arteries, arterioles, capillary beds, and veins begin to contract, slowing the flow of blood. The lactic acid formed during the race remains in the muscles, resulting in blood of an acid nature. It is advisable to remove this blood from muscle areas and replace it with blood of a higher pH. The best way to do this is by stimulating the circulation of the blood in a way that will not create further oxygen debts. Continuing to jog easily for 15 minutes or more after the race will do this. Lactic acid does not leave the body, but it is eventually changed into glycogen through various chemical processes within the body.

The warm-down also allows body temperature to return to normal slowly and lessens the possibility of chills. Take your warm-down seriously. A lot of runners fail to recognize its value, and as a result suffer from sore leg muscles, caused by the acidic blood remaining in the muscles and irritating muscle nerves. You can try to circulate acidic blood away from the muscles by massage, but I think it is far better to allow the heart to do it. You get the added benefit of breathing in large quantities of oxygen while you are jogging. Massage does have some value, but jogging is better.

In 1957, the Finish runner Salsola broke the world 1,500 meters record in unusual circumstances. He normally warmed up for 45 to 50 minutes, but this day he was resting in his hotel near the track in Turku and the person who was supposed to call him from the hotel forgot to do so. This was not discovered until the field was called together seven minutes before the race was to begin. There was a mad flurry and he was called and rushed to the track. He had been lying in bed and was quite warm. But he had no time for his customary long warm-up and was at the starting mark after only a few wind sprints. He won the race in world record time. His reaction was: "What would I have done with a proper warm-up?" The answer to that was that he never again ran that fast, despite his long warm-ups.

Chapter 10

Body Temperature and Exercise

Body temperature varies throughout the body. Body heat is lost through physiological processes that enable the blood to cool as it flows near the skin. Vaporization of sweat also cools the skin, dissipating body heat. When the air temperature is low, the blood vessels of the skin contract to diminish heat loss. When the temperature is high, or when exercise produces excess body heat, they dilate. At such times, more perspiration is secreted and evaporative heat loss is greater. The more you exercise, the more blood flows through the outer skin area and the more you perspire.

THE EFFECT OF HEAT

Strenuous exercise creates a demand for more blood in the muscles and the skin for cooling. The warmer the atmosphere, the greater the demand becomes. This pressure can exceed the capacity of the heart to increase cardiac output, causing nausea, dizziness, and even heat-stroke. If you're unaccustomed to strenuous exercise in the heat, you may be exposed to: (1) heat cramps through excessive loss of salt and water, which leads to neuromuscular breakdown; (2) heat exhaustion, through circulatory inadequacy caused by dehydration; or even (3) heat-stroke, a condition serious enough to be fatal because the temperature-controlling center of the brain becomes deranged. You can adapt yourself to exercising in the heat by carefully controlling and gradually lengthening the duration of exercise periods. This steadily improves circulation of blood to the arterioles in the skin, which brings about cooling.

Marathon runners must often race in hot conditions, where

body temperatures rise to extremes and dehydration is excessive. If they've been training in the heat, they can handle these conditions quite well, with good recovery afterwards. But those unaccustomed to the heat rarely finish, and are often in a distressed state of fatigue for some time after the race.

Jim Peter's marathon run in the 1954 Empire and Commonwealth Games in Vancouver is a classic example of a run by a fine marathon runner who came close to death through dehydration and circulatory failure. He was simply unprepared for competition in high heat.

People taking their first sauna bath usually feel extremely hot and even faint in temperatures around 175°F. But after a conditioning period of a few weeks, temperatures up to 245°F seem quite agreeable.

The body's temperature-regulating mechanism is most efficient, as I have shown during marathons in which I have been suffering from the effects of heat. Instead of using the customary sponge, I would upend a bucket of water over myself. The cooling effect was almost instantaneous and allowed me to run freely again. The fact that I could run my regular marathon-training courses 10 to 15 minutes faster on cool days demonstrated the degree to which the body metabolism is taxed in hot conditions.

I've often seen athletes, seeking to reduce weight, running distances on hot days in heavy clothing. They'll certainly rid their bodies of water and minerals. But, because they're limiting the volume of training they could do by the clothing they're wearing, they won't burn off as much fat as they might hope. In fact, a few hours after stopping they'll have replaced most of the liquid they lost and they'll essentially be back to where they began. They'd use up some of the fat if they ran with less clothing and kept the body temperature down so they could run farther and more intensely. They're also overlooking the fact that heavy clothing causes higher body temperatures. This draws blood from the working muscles to the skin for emergency cooling, impairing the efficiency of the muscles. Since it's necessary to do as large a volume of running as possible to develop general cardiac efficiency, anything that gets in the way of this should be avoided. So, when you're conditioning by running, wear only the clothing that is necessary. Any more retards movement, overheats the body, and reduces the benefits.

In high temperatures, it's possible to continue steady running for an hour or more, even when the thermometer is near 100°F. But the humidity must also be high, so that the moisture perspired remains on the skin surface to assist with cooling. If the humidity is low and the perspiration evaporates quickly, you'll suffer from dehydration and have difficulty.

Being the kind of person who has to find out these things for himself, I tried a run in Tucson, Arizona, when the temperature was 100° F and the humidity was less than 20 percent. I ran for about 20 minutes and then decided I had better stop. But, in Maracaibo, Venezuela, I trained regularly for six weeks, for an hour a day. Maracaibo is at sea level, and ten degrees from the equator, so the temperature is always high—100° to 120° F. In the middle of the day, when everyone else was taking a siesta, I used to run on the tarmac of an old airport. I could even do speed training for a full hour. Because the humidity was near 90 percent and I was always wet with perspiration, I suffered no ill-effects. I followed this program to accustom myself to the heat, so that I could sleep more easily at night, when it remained extremely hot.

The opposite applies when you're training in subzero temperatures. If there is moisture in the air when temperatures are around −5° to −40° F, it becomes almost impossible to train; you can ice your lungs. But if the humidity is below 20 percent, you can train in temperatures of −20° F for hours, provided the wind factor is not high and you're well wrapped up. As I explained earlier, I trained in Finland wearing the Finnish snow rig of two track suits—a suede outer one to stop the penetration of the cold, and a normal one inside that allowed air to pass through. This meant that a warm cushion of air was kept against the body. Apart from my cheeks, everything else was protected with woolen hat, muffler, gloves, and socks.

There's the formula: when the temperature is high, the humidity needs to be high; in lower temperatures, the humidity should also be low. If any other combination prevails, limit your training.

SALT LOSS

When you're training in a warm climate, or perspiring profusely, you have to replace salt as well as the water lost during exercise. In long-duration competition, such as marathons, you should take small quantities of a saline drink during the competition, before you feel the effects of dehydration. You must maintain blood balance and volume. Use a drink made of water, with a fruit extract flavoring, about a quarter of a teaspoonful of salt, and a dessertspoonful of glucose in each glass. The fruit extract is merely added to prevent vomiting, the normal reaction to swallowing salt. If you don't take salt with the water, the body won't retain the water, and you are likely to suffer from heat cramps. Dehydration lowers your physical efficiency by reducing the blood's velocity and volume of flow.

To counter salt loss during the training period, sprinkle a little extra on your food at mealtimes. Some runners take salt tablets, but I've found that these can cause nausea and gastric irritations. The extra sprinkle on food is ample for salt loss replacement, and it doesn't have undesirable aftereffects. Salt taken in small quantities is soon eliminated from the body in urine and perspiration. In larger doses, it is retained in body tissues and the bloodstream, and can create a state of *hyperchloremia*. The worst effect of this is hardening of the arteries, although this is a minor risk if you are in good physical condition.

This leads to the question of whether an athlete in an endurance competition should take larger than normal quantities of salt to build a reserve that can be called on quickly. If salt or other electrolytes are taken just before the start, there isn't enough time for the body to eliminate them through perspiration or urine. When you're running this helps to replace what you lose in the first few minutes of exercising.

Besides sodium chloride, many salts containing essential elements such as calcium are lost through perspiration. But numerous patented electrolyte drinks are available today to replace all of them. I recommend that any athlete who continually perspires in training and racing should take them regularly. They help in training, in racing, and in the recovery period. In effect, you're practically drinking back sweat—though of a better flavor.

On this question, I recently exchanged correspondence with Dr. J. C. Fitzherbert, of Wollongong, Australia. He had been treating the former Australian distance runner Dave Power in Wollongong Hospital for problems apparently related to the tremendous exertion he'd submitted himself to in recent years. Dr. Fitzherbert says it is possible to draw a distinction between biological fitness and physical fitness. Ideally, the two go together; but there are circumstances in which biological unfitness from severe physical effort can result in structural changes. Dr. Fitzherbert wrote:

> There seems no doubt that little attention is paid, by high-performance athletes, to some of the important effects of loss of the essential trace minerals. It has been established that high-performance athletes, as well as losing salt, lose large amounts of zinc and magnesium. The loss of these trace minerals results in very subtle changes in body physiology and biochemistry. Their loss can be exacerbated frequently by the diets of athletes, particularly when it is a diet high in protein, which leads to greater requirements of the essential trace elements.

> Replacement of the essential trace minerals is made even more difficult because of the deficiency of many of them in the soil and hence in the food which the athletes eat. Apart from the prevention of changes in physiology and biochemistry which the loss of these trace minerals can induce, their deficiency can lead to some loss of tensile strength, over the years, of collagen tissues, which is the basis for the not infrequent breakdown of athletes, sometimes when they are reaching the peak of their physical performance.

> The amount of zinc which is lost by high-performance athletes during training and competition cannot be replaced in their diet and their requirements could possibly be double or treble normal requirements.

Dr. Fitzherbert said he could not say whether ingesting large amounts of zinc and magnesium would actually increase performance. But it had been shown in patients with severe *claudication* [lameness] from peripheral vascular disease that increased blood flow into the muscles could develop over the months, with loss of pain when abundant amounts were ingested. An interesting side effect was that large amounts of zinc seemed to give protection from upper respiratory tract infection; while the person taking the zinc sulfate tablets might develop a cold, it was of short duration.

Dr. Fitzherbert recommended taking tablets containing 220 milligrams zinc sulfate, 50 milligrams magnesium sulfate, 5 milligrams vitamin B_1, and 5 milligrams vitamin B_2 three times a day during active training. He also warned that they could cause gastric irritation on an empty stomach, and should not, for that reason, be taken during actual competition. There was no reason, he said, why an athlete in light training should not take these once a day for three to four weeks. Dr. Fitzherbert continued:

Another interesting side effect of zinc, of course, is that it is the essential trace mineral of carbonic anhydrase and it is essential for the uptake of oxygen for haemoglobin. Zinc and magnesium play an essential role in the function of all cells, but particularly of the cardiac muscle.

Chapter 11

Diet and Exercise

Many athletes switch their normal diet before an important competition or at other times during their training, without giving careful thought to the effects of the changes. I have known athletes who changed normal eating habits and later complained they felt bad during competition, performed poorly, and realized too late what they had done. If you want to experiment with your diet, you should not wait until an important competition is pending and risk upsetting yourself. It is far better to try different foods for less important races or at less vital periods of training. That way you can test the effects without risking too much.

In countries with high standards of living, most athletes can maintain a balanced diet with few problems. In universities and other establishments where food is prepared in large quantities and the catering is for nonathletes rather than athletes in hard training, there may be certain vitamin and mineral deficiencies. This can be countered by taking vitamins, but, from my observations, I believe this is sometimes carried too far.

VITAMIN SUPPLEMENTS

Though there is endless debate about the value of vitamin supplements, you do need sufficient minerals and vitamins. Taking them in tablets is a good safeguard in situations where you cannot control the preparation or selection of your food. Remember, you can suffer physiological breakdown because of the pressure you are putting on yourself. Your vitamin and mineral requirement is higher than usual. But don't go to extremes and swallow every tablet you can get hold of.

The only athletes I trained who needed nutritional supplements were a few who were deficient in iron. But at that time New Zealand had plenty of fresh vegetables; most of us grew them in our own gardens. There was no lack of meat and other primary produce. Now, even in New Zealand, more processed food is being eaten; this evolution in eating habits must be considered. Everyone should evaluate his diet.

If a number of people sit down to identical meals, some will assimilate the necessary minerals from them, while others will suffer from deficiencies. Since it's an individual problem, it is, therefore, unwise to be too specific. But even in affluent societies athletes may need supplementary sources of minerals and vitamins in the form of tablets.

I honestly believe that the athletes I trained would not have run any faster if they had taken vitamin tablets. But I've noticed American athletes with bags full of multicolored vitamin pills. An American university physiologist told me he believed vitamin tablets were good for young babies or children up to about four or five. But he thought that young athletes with good available food sources were wasting their time with tablet-taking, and achieved little more than coloring their urine.

I was told the story of an athlete in an American college who was asked by his coach one day why he was looking so worried. The athlete, who had his little bag of colored tablets, said abjectly, "I've lost my little pink pill." And he went on scrabbling about on the ground looking for his pink pill to alleviate his worries. He had real faith in his pills. Maybe athletes gain the greatest benefit by believing they gain an advantage over other athletes by taking vitamins. It is a psychological rather than a physical benefit.

PRERACE DIET

It is important for runners who have accepted the marathon method of conditioning to increase their caloric intake. You cannot do this efficiently by eating additional bulky foods. They are harder to digest and place extra work on the digestive system. The best way is to eat more honey and glucose. These build the caloric intake to a high level easily without creating digestive problems. The body can store blood sugars in the liver and bloodstream.

I have proved in practice that it is highly beneficial to eat about 200 grams of sugar in the 36 hours preceding a competition. My athletes ate the glucose type of barley sugar, not chocolate, and began the intake on the Friday morning prior to competition, continuing through to the Saturday morning of the race. When I was visiting the Soviet Union, a Russian physiologist discussed this prerace sugar intake with me. He confirmed that they had proved scientifically that it worked. He found that 200 grams was the ideal amount, since more or less gave poor results.

When planning your diet, it is important to remember that the food you eat the day before you race provides most of the energy for the race and aids recovery. Forget about eating a steak the day of the race; it's the steak you eat the day before that will count.

The day of the race you should eat a breakfast of cereals, lightly cooked eggs (not hard-boiled), and tea, coffee, or any other drink you like. Avoid a heavy, fatty breakfast and give it plenty of time to digest. Lunch should be mainly carbohydrate, and there are various meals that meet this need without being too heavy. Honey sandwiches, of course, are ideal, as are baked beans.

Again, it's a question of determining what suits you individually. But it's not overly important. Many athletes would be better if they didn't eat anything at all. For instance, if they suffer from prerace tensions, their digestive systems could be upset by any food. The basic formula is to ingest protein to aid recovery from the race, but to confine yourself to carbohydrates on race day.

Drinking alcohol within 12 hours of a race is unwise. The alcohol is absorbed by the red blood cells, inhibiting the absorption of oxygen. But you can drink other liquids right up to race time. Even if you can hear the liquid sloshing about inside there will be no discomfort.

CARBOHYDRATE DIET

Carbohydrates are eaten by many middle- and long-distance runners before races to boost the amount of glycogen stored in the muscles above the normal level. The theory is that you do a long, hard training run 7 days before your event to depress the blood sugar level. From then until 4 days before the race, you keep the level down by eating almost exclusively fats or proteins to increase the muscles' ability to absorb sugar.

Training runs during this period are light and easy. On the afternoon of the fourth day before the race, you switch to a carbohydrate-enriched diet until the race. The body responds by storing up abnormal quantities of glycogen in the muscles, perhaps as much as three to four times the normal amount. The theory also states that you will feel very tired during the noncarbohdyrate period, but you must stick to the diet. I do not advise runners to use this method. If they are determined to, they should try it out in a race that is not too important. Don't make the common mistake of experimenting with this method first in a race you want to win.

In aerobic exercise, energy comes from a ratio of about 48 percent carbohydrates, 48 percent fatty acids, and 4 percent protein. In anaerobic exercise, the ratio is about 60 percent carbohydrates, 25 percent fatty acids, and 15 percent protein. There is thus an increase in the burning of carbohydrates in competition that calls for anaerobic effort. It's that fact that has led athletes to try to increase the amount of glycogen in the body to offset the quick depletion of their energy. But it is debatable whether the body can store extra glycogen through this method, and it can also lead to other problems. There is a need for fatty acids and proteins; if they are not sufficient, the runner on the carbohydrate diet can suffer from dizziness and experience greater muscle soreness afterward.

My advice is this: if you want to build up blood sugars to the maximum, take a light laxative six days before the race so that your bowels are loosened a little, but not a lot. The laxative stimulates the liver to produce the maximum amount of glycogen the body can contain. Eat the meals you are normally accustomed to and, during the two days preceding the competition, eat up to 200 grams of sugar, glucose, or honey. I prefer honey because it is mainly fructose and easy to digest. The sugars consumed in the final two days add an abundance of energy without upsetting the balance of fatty acid, protein, and carbohydrate. To attempt more than that is supercompensation, which is the same as trying to put five liters into a four-liter bucket. At this point you should be training lightly and aerobically, with little use of energy.

Sugar is harder to digest, so don't eat it within 3 to 4 hours of your competition. While the liver is processing the sugar into glycogen it will not release the quantity of glucose required into the bloodstream. If extra sugar is eaten, either as glucose, fructose, or galactose, in excess of immediate needs, the liver and other tissues convert it into fat for energy later.

The French physiologist Claude Bernard discovered that the glucose content of blood entering the liver just after a meal has a much higher concentration of sugar than blood leaving the liver. Between meals, liver glycogen is reconverted into glucose, so that the concentration of glycogen in the blood leaving the liver is much higher than in the blood entering the liver. Bernard also found that the liver maintains a more or less constant glucose concentration in the blood throughout the day.

It is important during your training to maintain a reasonable intake of glucose or fructose to supplement the diet. This provides sufficient energy without overworking the digestive system with extra-large quantities of food. Honey, which contains about 78 percent fructose, 20 percent water, and 2 percent of a few minerals and vitamins, is practically a complete energy food. It is an ideal carbohydrate, with the added advantage of being easy to digest.

Chapter 12

Running Equipment

CLOTHING

The clothing you wear will be governed by the conditions in which you train and race. In warmer climates, you don't need track suits for conditioning training or for much of the track training. But you do need a waterproof Windbreaker with a zip up the front to keep you dry and warm should it rain heavily. The zip can be used to control the temperature in the Windbreaker.

When possible, it is much better and easier to train with light clothing so you are not hampered by a track suit, which can make you too hot and, in wet weather, can be too heavy. In cold climates, however, a track suit is a necessity for winter training. The weight of the suit will be determined by the severity of the cold.

When temperatures are below 0°F, it pays to wear two track suits, as we did in Finland—one of material that allows air to pass through beneath one of material that prevents the passage of air. This keeps the cold air out and forms a cushion of warm air between the outer suit and your body. With this outfit, you can run in −40°F for 2 hours or more without trouble. Talk to other runners about the types of materials their suits are made of before you buy your own.

Hooded and warm top shirts are useful for training in cold, dry weather and for warming up on cold days.

Your running shorts should fit comfortably and not drag on your legs when your knees come up. If they do, you can expect problems on wet days when the drag is accentuated. For men, athletic supports are a thing of the past; they can cause chafing of the crotch. It is much better, if you do not have shorts with a

101

sewn-in support, to use women's briefs. I recall being in a training camp at Woodville, in northeast Texas, in 1970 when about thirty of us went for a 22-mile run on a hot, humid day. There were broad smiles of amusement when the American boys saw me changing into a pair of women's cotton briefs. But at the end of the run I was the only one smiling because I was the only one not chafed. The next day, about thirty runners traipsed into the local women's clothing store and asked for female briefs. The woman attendant looked alarmed until it was explained why so many men wanted women's underclothes. She did great business.

SHOES

Shoes are probably the most important item of equipment, and it's important when you're buying to try the complete pair. Stand up and walk in them, feeling for any pressure points that could later cause problems. They should not bite into the heels at the achilles tendons; they should not be too tight across the joints of your feet; and they should not touch the ends of your toes, because once you begin running your feet can swell and move a little, causing you to lose toenails. There should not be any pressure points.

Once you are sure the shoes fit, you should check that they have good rubber soles to protect you from the impact of the hard surfaces you may train on. If the heels have been cut away, they will be no good for road training, because when you run downhill you'll need that rubber on the back edges of the heels to take the jarring. This is a vital part of the road-training shoe. Some shoe manufacturers slope the back of the heels because it causes less wear, but it doesn't protect the runner.

If you're selecting training shoes for running in low temperatures, where icy surfaces may be expected, it is advisable to have soles that are semisoft for better traction. Most rubbers are temperature-sensitive, and will harden in cold weather, reducing traction and offering less cushioning against jarring.

When selecting track shoes for middle- and long-distance running, it is best to buy shoes with rubber wedges on the heels to take the jarring of hard tracks and to ease the strain on the tendons and muscles at the back of the legs.

For cross-country running, it is best to get a pair of spiked shoes of a more solid and stronger construction than you would use on the track to get you over muddy terrain and rough ground. These conditions can quickly wreck lighter track shoes. The type of shoes used by orienteering runners—with a series of small rubber studs on the soles—are ideal for most cross-country courses. They give good grip for running down slippery slopes, and are designed for hard wear on rough ground.

If you buy spiked shoes, try to get shoes that have a good placement of screw-in spikes. You need spikes as near to the toe as possible, since you drive forward from this point, and thus need maximum traction. Spikes should be under the outer edge of the forepart of the shoe because your feet roll onto the outside of the joints, particularly when you are going around bends.

Place the laces in such a way that when they are tightened they do not pull down on the sinews and the metatarsals of the top of the foot. Bring the laces up parallel with the foot, across to the hole directly opposite, and then underneath on the same side to the hole two places nearer the ankle. Don't cross them the usual diagonal way. A simple matter like incorrect lacing can prevent the foot from functioning freely, because it is forced to strain against restrictions that can cause damage.

Watch shoe heel wear closely. Excessive wear leads to stress right through the leg and hip, and can also cause bone damage.

STOPWATCHES

If you are a middle- or long-distance runner, never buy a stopwatch without a full 60-second dial. The 30-second ones can lead to confusion, particularly if you're trying to time more than one runner in trials or races. Some watches don't clearly show the seconds and split seconds; it pays to have a dial that is easily read. Some watches have a *splits hand* that can be stopped and started without stopping the main hand. This is invaluable for getting accurate lap and other split times.

Stopwatches are expensive, so it pays to give this a lot of thought before you choose the one most suitable for your purpose. If cared for, they can last indefinitely. The digital types now available leave no doubts about actual elapsed times and are an improvement on the standard type. However, most of them are more expensive. If you want to time accurately while you're running, it is best to use an electronic stopwatch, as other types may be affected by your movement.

Part III

Special Training

Chapter 13

Young Runners

From my experience and from research and experience in many countries, seven seems to be the age at which boys and girls can begin absorbing large amounts of long-distance running without any undesirable side effects. Youngsters under fifteen can handle considerable aerobic training because their capacity to use oxygen in relation to their body weight is greater than an adult's. However, they usually have highly sensitive nervous systems and cannot stand much anaerobic training. It's not unusual to hear of boys and girls of ten to twelve running weekly mileages of up to 120 and even 160 kilometers and continuing to improve athletically.

Competitive racing does not harm youngsters of any age, provided the races are kept to sprints over short distances not more than 200 meters, or middle- and long-distance races of 800 meters or more. Prolonged sprints of 300 to 400 meters can cause problems because the oxygen debts incurred through sustained speed running are often more than youngsters can handle. These distances can cause young runners to be sick, to black out, or to suffer distress afterward. Most youngsters can run 200 meters quite fast, but by then they have developed a large oxygen debt. In a 400-meter race, this would mean they would be exhausted at the finishing straight, where they might force themselves to overdo it. The 800-meter races are a different story. Youngsters recognize this is not a sprint, and settle into a pace they can manage without undue distress.

I recall watching a schoolgirls' 800-meter race in Auckland in 1973, which was open to girls of thirteen to nineteen. There was no other middle-distance race for the thirteen-year-old girls. So, if

107

they were not fast enough for the shorter events like the 400 meters, and they wanted to compete, they were forced to race against girls much older. On this occasion, a small girl of thirteen collapsed after the first lap because the pace set by the older girls was far too fast for her.

I remarked to a teacher on the planning committee for the race that she was responsible for the child's condition since her committee had not assembled a realistic athletic program. It was forcing youngsters to compete in events unsuitable for them, and placing too much stress on them. In the following years, I was pleased to note that the school's program included more middle-distance races for the younger girls.

However, there is still a need for longer races, such as 3,000 meters for girls of all secondary-school ages. How else will the younger and slower girls be encouraged to train for, and participate in, a sport that can only do them good?

New Zealand youngsters have always run cross-country from an early age. Boys are into 3,000- to 5,000-meter runs from about eight onward. This may seem a tremendous demand, but we've found that provided their hearts are sound they'll have no problem. Sustained speed, not sustained running, can cause damage. Emphasis on speed has wrecked many potential champions over the years in more countries than New Zealand.

I always remember the words of Gundar Haegg's coach: "If you can get a boy in his teens and encourage him to train and not race until he is matured, then you have laid the foundations of an Olympic champion." I believe that sums up the whole thing. Encourage young athletes, but don't force them. Let them play at athletics and with athletics. If you encourage training from that perspective, their capacity for exercise, and the benefits they draw from it, will astound you.

Boys in New Zealand enjoy running in packs over hills and through valleys, jumping creeks and fences, enjoying fresh air and sunshine in a sport that recognizes none of the confines of the measured field. I have not seen one of them fall in an exhausted heap to be picked up and carried away. But all of them are conditioning themselves for more serious running later on.

One of the great advantages of cross-country running is that parents cannot follow alongside, urging young runners to run faster and more intensely than they are physically and mentally prepared to do. Parental influence on sport can be a wonderful contribution, but it can also be dangerous and destructive. Too many parents are more interested in seeing their children excel than encouraging them merely to enjoy themselves. Many parents force their children to demonstrate superiority at the expense of the children themselves.

Schedule training can be successfully applied to young runners. In Auckland, many youngsters regularly include in their weekly running the 35-kilometer Waitakere Ranges circuit, over which Snell, Halberg, Magee, and my other athletes trained. They do this at their own pace and without discomfort. This is a steep hill training circuit, which is regarded as formidable even by mature runners. But young runners enjoy it, because the only pressure they apply is the pressure they choose for themselves; that is always within their capacity.

Chapter 14

Training for Women

It has taken a long time for administrators to promote, or even allow, women's middle- and long-distance events. Even now, there is resistance in some countries to women running further than 1,500 meters. There is no physiological reason why women should not run marathons, let alone 3,000 meters or further in track races. Yet in many countries, women whose talents lie in the longer events are barred from competing. The 1980 Moscow Olympics, however, will feature a 3,000-meter race for women.

The 800-meter event for women was reintroduced into the Olympic Games amid a storm of controversy over the possible ill-effects of vigorous competition on females. It has now become generally accepted that women can race this distance. The 800-meter final at the 1964 Tokyo Olympics was one of the most exciting track and field events.

Today, we are witnessing many fine performances by European women, particularly from the Soviet Union, East and West Germany, and Bulgaria. Most of these women have approached their training seriously, running around 200 kilometers a week, and conditioning themselves so that they do not carry excess weight. Women runners in many other countries, however, are not doing a sufficient volume of training, and do not watch their diets closely enough. Russian and German women have the added advantage that they are getting more scientific assistance and encouragement.

In the future, women's world records for the middle- and long-distance events will continue to be lowered as more women train harder and more scientifically in a field that is still relatively new to most of them.

Some women are already running the 42-kilometer marathon in times under 2:40, and will more than likely get under 2:30 before long. There is no reason why this should not be so. There will be growing pressure on administrators for more of the longer distance competitions to be officially recognized Olympic events. These could eventually include the marathon and the 2,000-meter steeple-chase. I have seen women steeplechasing and they can perform well. The increasing interest of women in these competitions should make for exciting racing in the future.

EFFECTS OF EXERCISE

There are many fallacies surrounding the influence of exercise and sports participation on menstruation. It has been generally accepted that women should avoid vigorous activity before, during, and immediately after their periods. This general conclusion, however, is not based on fact. Menstruation is a biological phenomenon, placing a particular burden on the blood production system. It was therefore assumed that any additional physical stress on the organism during this period would overload the physiological functions, and thus disturb the cycle in some harmful way.

It has been shown that changes do take place during menstruation, but these changes can be either beneficial or harmful. In other words, it is purely an individual matter; an activity that upsets one woman need not upset another. Research has shown that vigorous activity, even to the point of voluntary fatigue, benefits as many as it harms in terms of length and volume of menstrual flow.

It is now accepted that the effect of exercise is related to the mental and physical characteristics of the female. Restrictions of physical activity during menstruation should not be generally applied, but should rather be treated individually.

Research suggests that anyone who measures up to the following general requirements should not need to restrict activity during menstruation:

1. enjoys good health
2. is physically fit and in condition to do the activity
3. does not perform exercises that require excessive abdominal contraction and compression, or cause excessive shock or bouncing

4. does not perform activities that require explosive action such as the shot put and discus

5. avoids extreme heat and cold

6. is not coerced into participation against her will

There is no biological or medical foundation for the belief that certain sports have harmful effects on the maternal function. All evidence now indicates that the female receives benefits from competitive sport and exercise, particularly during delivery and in the postpartum period.

Females have a lighter and weaker build, and less capacity for physical performance than males. They have lighter and smaller bones, smaller muscles in proportion to the total body weight, and less muscle bulk. Most females are about one-third less strong than males in individual muscle size and total strength. The cardiopulmonary reserve capacity of the female is about two-thirds that of the male. She does not, therefore, obtain the same oxygen intake, ventilation volume, and cardiac output as the male during physical performance.

Women, however, have the physiological capacity to perform the same types of movement and engage in the same physical activities as men, limited only by intensity and duration. At her own level, a female can match a male in activities requiring speed, strength, endurance, and skill. Most scientific evidence today indicates that physically fit females in good health can generally participate in competitive sports without harmful effects. But there are exceptions, and anyone in doubt should seek medical consultation and supervision.

TRAINING PROGRAMS

When I first trained young men in their early teens, I was cautious about the amount of training I could give them. I knew how much a man could stand and still improve, but I didn't know what a youth could take without impairing his performance. After years of experimentation, I concluded that boys could run up to 160 kilometers a week with beneficial results. But it is essential that speed is controlled to an economic level, and that they do considerable supplementary jogging as well.

The same is true of the training of women. At their own level, they can train just as long as men. Young women beginning training should jog daily on grass; parks and golf courses are ideal. The soft surface allows muscles to condition comfortably while the respiratory and circulatory systems are being toned. Fifteen minutes a day is enough at first. But once the expected initial soreness has disappeared from the muscles, the time should be increased to half an hour a day, and then to an hour.

This is easier than you may think, since the body reacts to training with a rapid improvement in stamina and general condition. Cross-country training and racing should be brought into the system early. This should occur before the runner progresses to a conditioning schedule, resistance training, and track work. The latter places greater demands on the body's resources and depends for success on the quick recovery that stamina and strong condition provide.

Schedules for women are included in this book, but there is not one specifically for the marathon. Women training for this event should modify it something like this:

Monday	Steady running, 1 hour
Tuesday	Easy fartlek running, ½ hour
Wednesday	Steady running, 1½ hours
Thursday	Steady running, 1 hour
Friday	Easy fartlek running, 1½ hours
Saturday	Steady running, 1½ hours
Sunday	Steady running, 1½ hours

The fartlek or speed play should include more stride-outs than sprint work. That is, during a half-hour run at an even pace, the runner should stride out periodically over any distance up to 200 meters, should increase speed on uphill slopes, and stride out on downhill slopes.

Chapter 15

Strictly for Joggers

Since 1960, thousands of people around the world have taken to jogging as a means of achieving physical fitness, and hopefully prolonging a healthy and happy life. Thousands of hours have been spent researching the reasons for the good results from jogging.

I began to recommend jogging for all ages in the early 1960s, while looking for the right formula for training competitive athletes for middle- and long-distance events. I discovered that long, easy running brought me and my pupils remarkable development in basic fitness, in the capacity to absorb the punishment of competition running, and in the ability to improve performance. I then had no clear idea why this happened. I only knew that my stamina and endurance increased phenomenally, my pulse rate fell, and my tirelessness enabled me to go on searching, working— and running.

In recent years, sports medicine experts and physiologists in many countries have put the jogging theories under scrutiny, and found that jogging is second only to cross-country skiing as the best exercise for developing general cardiac efficiency, with minimal risk to the individual. Cardiac efficiency is the factor that enables us to live longer and better.

If you are a beginner, tell your doctor what you want to do, and get his blessing before you work out further. If your cardiac condition is such that applying any strain to the heart could be dangerous, you should know first; only your doctor can tell you that.

PHYSIOLOGICAL BENEFITS

Jogging increases your oxygen uptake and allows your body metabolism to function better. It eases duress on the heart by increasing the oxygen content of the blood. This means the heart needs to pump much less blood to various parts of the body and through the coronary arteries to do relatively the same amount of work it did before.

Regular jogging increases pulmonary ventilation, or the efficiency of the alveoli of the lungs, allowing more air to reach the blood that is pumped into the lungs. It also increases the number of red cells, and the myoglobin and hemoglobin content of the blood and muscles. This allows even more oxygen to be extracted from the air entering the lungs. The increased oxygen intake allows the heart to function still more efficiently, reflected by a drop in the pulse rate.

First phase of jogging. This phase involves taking the pressure off the heart by increasing the oxygen content of the blood. The blood's red cells are constantly renewed over a six-week period. If you create a fatigue rate (making yourself a little tired through exercise) the metabolic response is to increase both the renewal rate and the quality of the red cells during that cycle, leading to better blood tone. The minute and stroke volumes of the heart steadily increase. This means that progressively more blood can be pumped to the respiratory system each minute to take in even greater quantities of oxygen when needed.

Second phase of jogging. Once the oxygen-carrying capacity of the blood is raised, you can place greater work loads on the heart. This means that, as a jogger, you can comfortably run faster and farther without any apparent increase in effort. If you maintain a faster pace and cover more miles, you once again increase the pressure on the cardiovascular and circulatory system. If you maintain this pressure for 15 minutes or longer, it begins to work on under-developed arteries, arterioles, capillaries, and veins, developing a more efficient circulatory network. Blood flows more freely and the pressure is counteracted again as a natural metabolic reaction. The heart's work becomes easier and the pulse rate falls even lower.

This secondary phase of jogging should only be entered after the oxygen uptake has been improved through easy exercise at the aerobic level. If your oxygen uptake level is low, as it probably will be if you haven't exercised regularly, overeffort quickly takes you out of the aerobic state into the anaerobic state. Then you will rapidly develop lactic acid in the bloodstream, a cause of neuromuscular breakdown in large quantities. It can upset the heart's rhythm and lead to the very thing we're aiming to avoid— heart trouble.

If your oxygen uptake level is half that of your next-door neighbor and you both go digging in your garden for half an hour, your heart will need to pump nearly twice as much blood as his does. Your heart will be under strain; you'll be running into an oxygen debt and accumulating lactic acid; you probably won't get as much digging done; and you'll feel it later while he's comfortable and relaxed, benefiting from his exercise.

Here's another example of oxygen debt and neuromuscular breakdown that you can try for yourself. Jump up and hang from a horizontal bar. Eventually, your fingers will become numb, your muscles will protest, and you'll be forced to let go. The reason is simply that lactic acid accumulates due to lack of oxygen to the muscles holding you up.

So, if you are a novice jogger, train like one. Exercise well within your fitness level and your capacity to exercise for at least 6 weeks. Your body will tell you those limits; take notice of them. If, after a few minutes of quiet jogging, you feel like stopping for a walk to get your breath, stop and walk. Don't try to keep on running. By stopping, you'll be helping your system to improve. By running on, you'll be slowing improvement.

Third phase of jogging. This phase of jogging, and its effect on the oxygen uptake, is brought about through still greater muscular efficiency. If muscles are exercised regularly for long periods without rest—1½ hours or more—the capillary beds are subjected to great pressure and encouraged to develop. Totally new capillary beds form. This results in sharply increased muscular efficiency in the use of oxygen.

Numerous accomplished joggers—many over 60—have applied this system patiently and carefully. They have surprised everyone by the ease with which they can jog 20 miles or more, when, as little as a year earlier, they could not cover a quarter-mile at a walking pace without reaching exhaustion.

Fundamentally, increased oxygen uptake involves an increase in the intake, transportation, and utilization of oxygen within your bloodstream. Its end result is increased metabolic efficiency, which removes strain from the heart and gives you increased energy. You won't tire so quickly, either physically or mentally, because the higher oxygen content of your blood proves the efficiency of the central nervous system. This improves concentration, coordination, and reflex actions. We've shown that jogging can reduce one's golf handicap by ten strokes, simply because you can concentrate, coordinate, react more efficiently, and keep tiredness at bay.

You'll look different too. Improved metabolism slows down the aging process, the physical and mental deterioration of the human body. Fit people don't look as old as people of the same age who live sedentary lives, with a lower oxygen uptake.

YOUR JOGGING PROGRAM

So let's get started, bearing in mind that for the next 6 weeks you should run for no longer than 15 minutes at a time—preferably every day of the week, and certainly no fewer than 4 days a week or on alternate days. There are few of us who cannot spend 1 to 1¾ hours a week to make sure we live better and longer. Remember, you should run aerobically during this time. Your running will be economical, jogging quietly along, well within your limits, breathing out carbon dioxide and sweating out salts and minerals.

Don't forget to gain your doctor's approval first, and then seek out a park or a quiet, relatively flat area to begin jogging. Never overdo the exercise; aim to reach a state of pleasant tiredness, not exhaustion. Never finish with a sprint to show how good you are. If your breathing becomes labored, walk until you've recovered enough to feel like jogging more. You can run too fast but you can never run too slowly to gain in cardiac efficiency. The more running you do at this easy pace the better.

If you experience some preliminary muscle soreness, don't stop. Keep moving very easily, preferably on grass. Your body will concentrate on healing the sore areas, but only if you keep working at it.

Well-soled shoes are essential to eliminate jarring, which can cause trouble in the leg joints and the back. Good shoes are costly, but they're a worthwhile investment and about the only big expense you have to face to keep yourself in condition.

A sensible diet should be followed by decreasing the intake of carbohydrates and keeping the calorie intake at a reasonable level. This doesn't involve adopting any fads. Your diet will probably change naturally as you become more fit and your body tells you what it needs and what it will no longer accept. It's wise to stop eating sugar and other processed foods. If possible, use honey instead of sugar. Stick to whole-meal flour.

And if you're a smoker, you'll find out why you shouldn't be. Where fitness is concerned, smoking is the worst thing you can do. But your own growing appreciation of the benefits of fitness will diminish your apparent need for cigarettes. Smoking pollutes the body, and forces your heart, lungs, and other organs to work harder to counter its effects. It also lowers oxygen uptake, the very thing we're trying to improve.

You'll lose excess weight and reduce blood cholesterol levels gradually. However, cholesterol levels vary from one person to another, and can be quite high in people who don't eat foods such as fats, which are generally responsible for cholesterol buildup.

The golden rule to follow is to be regular and gentle with your exercise. A little often is better than a lot occasionally. Choose your jogging time to suit yourself. Any time of day or night is fine, except for the 2 or 3 hours following a major meal. Let your digestion do its work first, since it makes a demand for the oxygen you need for jogging.

Part IV

International Coaching

Chapter 16

Coaching in Mexico

I approached my first overseas coaching appointment, with Mexico in 1965, with considerable excitement. Because of the success I had achieved with my small group of New Zealand runners, none of whom was a superman, I could imagine the possibilities of having a whole nation to work with. There is no country in the world that does not have the potential to develop successfully. And, because Mexico was hosting the 1968 Olympic Games, I went there with both the desire and the intention of doing a good job for them.

POLITICAL STUMBLING BLOCKS

It didn't take long to assess the high potential of Mexican athletes. But soon I realized I couldn't hope to get the cooperation, politically, that I needed.

General José de J. Clark, who was in charge of Olympic preparations, was the one I had to talk to when I wanted anything for the program I envisioned for my athletes. This was not easy. I would join the people waiting to see him and, invariably, he would arrive two or three hours late. I didn't take kindly to it, or to the curt manner he adopted in his dealings, as if we were all subordinates in his army. I tried playing him at his own game—I made an appointment and arrived three hours late. I was still five minutes earlier than the general. And it all proved a waste of time going to see him. The United States coaches there all warned me at the outset that I should just flow with the stream and accept the situation. The general had already established through the press that he had brought the best coaches in the world to prepare the Mexican Olympic team, and that the responsibility for success or failure was ours.

There was the problem of suitable running shoes, for example. I discovered that I was taking my athletes out on runs of 20 kilometers or longer on hot roads with inferior shoes. Some had virtually no soles to them, and they were unable to get new ones because the money allocated for shoes was going to the private bank accounts of various officials.

I arranged with my interpreter, José Contrares, who had been a roommate of Jim Ryun at the University of Kansas, to meet the manager of the Canada Shoe Company. This was to take place at Guadalajara, about 20 kilometers from Mexico City. I outlined the problem to the manager, and explained how important it was to Mexican prestige that all our athletes should have the right shoes for training and competition.

"I'll do everything I can to help," the manager assured me. "Tell us what you want and we will make it."

We stayed a few days in Guadalajara, at the shoe company's expense, while some sample shoes were prepared. They were excellent, and when we said so, the manager told us to take a sample to the general and tell him the company would supply as many as we needed without charge. I showed the shoe to General Clark and told him of the offer. He tossed the shoe on his desk and said, "We don't need any free shoes."

I told the story to the pentathlon coach and he laughed. "What about me?" he asked. "We don't have any horses to ride. Or guns to shoot. Or a pool to swim in. What hope have I got of training my boys? You haven't really got a problem at all."

I did get some cooperation, however. I was supplied with buses whenever I wanted to take my runners up into the hills or out on the highway for training runs. The first of these trips was nearly 8,000 meters up for a 32-kilometer run in arid cactus country. The bus dropped us at the starting point and then followed with our clothing, food, and drinks. But it had to keep stopping to pick up the athletes. One after the other, they developed blisters, sore heels, muscle problems, and so on until, at the end, I was the only one left running ahead of a busload of relaxing athletes.

I announced that next time the bus door would be locked at the start of the run and would stay locked until the finish. Anyone who developed leg or other troubles would have to keep running or walking, and there would be nothing to eat or drink until the end. A few put the ultimatum to the test. It was fascinating to watch the limps and hobbles vanish as it dawned on them that I meant what I had said. All of them ran all the way.

They were good lads. One of them was Juan Martinez, who ran fourth in the 5,000 meters and fifth in the 10,000. Another, Alfredo Penaloza, was eighteenth in the marathon. One runner improved to set the Mexican 800-meter record. They proved that the tactics were worthwhile.

Most of them were from the villages of the Toluca area and had been brought up frugally on corn, chicken, and a local drink called pulque, a fermented cactus juice. This potent drink is unexpectedly high in mineral and vitamin value, but it was banned from the Olympic village. So when we were out on our distance runs I let the runners stop in any village we passed through and have their beloved pulque.

They developed as very good and fast runners, and they should have succeeded in the middle distances as well as the longer races. But this is a potential that can only be developed over a systematic three-year program, something I could not get the officials to appreciate and which I was not destined to carry through.

There were other problems, too, that I could do nothing about. Many of the boys were in the army, and most were of a particular Catholic faith that encouraged them to marry young and beget an endless stream of children. By twenty-two, they had often fathered five or six. And, to make their army life bearable, they had to pay some of their wages regularly into a fund established by the officers for the officers. Those who didn't found themselves on latrine duty, weekend exercises, or some other disciplinary punishment until they toed the line. They lived with financial problems that made it virtually impossible for them to get anywhere, especially in athletics, on their own. And with the problems I faced, I couldn't help them much.

I did have one failure in Mexico. We were told there were Indians living in the mountains who could run 100 kilometers without stopping. These were the guys, we decided, we could train to win the marathon for us. So we arranged a trial marathon for them and brought them down from the mountains. Unfortunately, the local officials knew nothing about organizing marathons. When they were told that feeding stations were required, they happily went ahead and organized a complete banquet. The Indians were accustomed to living simply, so when they reached the first feeding station and saw the food spread out for them, that is where they stopped.

MY DEPARTURE

I stuck it out for eight months of my 3-year contract and then had another meeting with General Clark. I managed to bluff him into agreeing that my contract should be declared null and void. Then I made plans for a quick exit from Mexico.

I knew that, because of my reputation, my departure from the scene could cause the general some embarrassment. I also knew that an Italian cycling coach, who had earlier caused embarrassment by becoming involved with the girlfriend of an Olympic committee member, had been dealt with drastically. He had been bundled out of bed in the middle of the night with a pistol at his head, forced to sign a statement breaking his contract, and dumped on the next plane out.

I quietly booked a flight to Canada instead of New Zealand and was gone before the officials were aware of it. It was depressing to leave like this. I left behind a group of young men who could not have been more dedicated to my program. Some of them wept when they farewelled me at the airport. I knew they could have done wonderful things for Mexico in 1968 if only we could have got the official help we needed. It was galling to know the money that had been allocated would never reach them.

I was met in Canada by the press, and I told them frankly what was happening in Mexico. Everything was behind schedule for the 1968 Olympics. The rowing course, for instance, was still a swamp. The press took this up with gusto, and three weeks later General Clark was deposed as Mexico's Olympic head, and a new man, a good one, was installed.

Chapter 17

The Finnish Experience

The first high point of my career came at the 1960 Rome Olympics. There, after all the experimenting and the development of my training program, we had final proof of the system. This came about through trial and error, with the criticism and opposition of various people—particularly when I had an 800-meter runner training and racing over marathon distances.

I think the greatest race, as far as my athletes were concerned, was Murray Halberg's 5,000 meters. It was one of the deciding factors in establishing that we'd finally balanced the program. Everything went exactly as planned. Murray won the race through good control and an understanding of the weaknesses of the other athletes. We had calculated these weaknesses on the basis of the faults and fallacies in the training methods they were using.

We evaluated everything carefully. We knew exactly what physiological reactions other athletes were getting from their training; we knew their failings; we knew Halberg's strengths; and we knew the time to use those strengths against other athletes' weaknesses. The race went like clockwork.

The next true highlight, of course, was the victory of the Finns in the 1972 Munich Olympics. This, however, was bridged from Rome by several years in which my runners totally dominated the middle- and long-distance running scene, setting national and world records. After Rome, we enjoyed a period when my team of runners was assured of winning all the races we chose to win because we alone were employing the best system.

I wasn't directly associated with the Finns in 1972, but the program I had instituted for them earlier gave them the kind of results

I had achieved in Rome. The Finns carried out the fundamental training correctly, they balanced everything nicely, and they trained specifically for the Olympics. Their eventual success came through the systematic approach they adopted as a result of my appointment there.

THE QUESTION OF BLOOD DOPING

It's an interesting, if unfortunate, fact that wherever you find success you find critics who try to detract from it. The Finns were accused of replacing their athletes' blood with higher-oxygenated blood. This accusation was repeated after Lasse Viren came back in Montreal to win the 5,000- and 10,000-meter gold medals for the second time. This is absurd, but some people believe it because it's what they want to hear. If the Finns had taken some of the blood from Viren and Vassala and put in into some other athletes, there might have been something in this theory. But these men were well trained, and they'd won numerous races before Munich to prove it.

My first association with Viren was during my term as the Finns' chief coach, when he was in the A-grade group (under eighteen-year-olds). Viren came into the training center at Viremaki for a few days with his coach and mentor. I should explain that the Finns bring their most promising athletes of various age-groups and their coaches together at regular intervals to maintain interest and to be sure training is progressing along accepted lines.

Viren was a most promising runner at that age, and was already the Finnish age-group champion. Through continued systematic training he has developed into the greatest distance runner the world has seen. His four Olympic gold medals prove it; but some newsmen and even athletes have suggested he won them because of *blood doping*. Blood doping means that an athlete trains, preferably at a high altitude, to improve blood toning so it becomes more oxygen-rich. A pint or so is then taken from him and put into storage for reinjection later. When he returns to sea level just before the important race, the supposedly richer blood is returned to his body, thus improving performance by increasing the number of oxygen-carrying blood cells available.

But knowing Viren's ability, he would only have needed systematic training to beat other runners in the 1976 Olympics. Such is his talent and ability to apply himself that at that time he could

Dick Quax leading Lasse Viren, who won the 5,000 meters at the 1976 Montreal Olympics. (Photograph by Mark Shearman.)

have beaten anyone. Generally, athletes who train for marathons
have excellent blood tone. So it is unlikely that their blood at high
altitudes would be much richer in oxygen than their blood during
normal training at sea level. Athletes with low blood counts who
continually won important races have puzzled physiologists. Even
when athletes changed diets and received injections of iron and
vitamin B-12, their blood counts remained the same.

The most important aspect of endurance training is not so much
assimilation and transportation of oxygen, but its utilization. For
instance, any unfit person can go to a high altitude and gain in
blood tone. But when they return to sea level they do not run faster simply because of better blood toning. They still need to transport and use the extra oxygen in their muscles. The value of extra
blood volume is debatable and limited.

If Viren had utilized blood doping—though I am sure he did
not—then what about the other Finnish runners? How do you explain their performances?

A great deal was made of Viren's comparatively unimportant
efforts between Olympics. After Munich he suffered a leg injury
that needed an operation. He tried to train without the operation,
but was finally forced to have it. Then he took his time about re-
covering and building up again. He approached his training for
Montreal the same way he did before Munich. Because he knew
how to train for big competitions, he was able to step out and beat
opponents unfamiliar with such training techniques. He was immediately criticized by a disgruntled few, including some he beat in
the finals and would beat again and again. He should have been
lauded by everyone. My hope is that we will see Viren again at the
Moscow Olympics.

The Finns' success at Munich was to the credit of the great
coaches Pentekavonen and Kaari Sinkonnen, who were responsible
to a large extent for these athletes becoming Olympic champions.

ARRIVAL IN FINLAND

I arrived in Finland in April 1966 with no idea of their athletic
problems or why runners were not succeeding, and I was con-
fronted with people looking for fast results. Neither the reasons
for the problems, nor the solutions were easy. I later learned that
though the problems and answers vary from country to country,
the basic handling of them doesn't change much. It's always tricky.

I found that Finland spent a lot of money on sports promotion. The people administering the funds were mainly business executives. It was evident they felt their business reputations were jeopardized by their inability to succeed as administrators—in that they weren't producing world champions. Since they were handling a lot of of money, it was assumed that they should be successful. Athletics is the main Finnish summer pastime, and the pressure was on from the people and the press for Finland to produce another Nurmi.* But all they were getting were athletes running way at the back of the international fields.

I soon realized that Finland's basic problem was that the young Finns had lost their toughness. They weren't out training in the winter like they should have been. I had had preconceived notions of hardy Scandinavians spending winters out on their skis and making use of the snow with scornful disregard of the conditions. But when I went out to learn skiing, I hardly ever saw a Finn. They were all inside, watching other people skiing on television. An affluent society was emerging in Finland and the tough young men and women of Finland had vanished into it. I sought out the older runners, like Heino, one of the world's best postwar 10,000-meter runners, and, sadly, these men concurred that the Finns were becoming soft. They saw this as a bad omen for a small country, with the Soviet Union on one border, Sweden on another, and no military alliances to provide protection. Finland needed a young, strong, healthy nationalistic backbone, and it wasn't getting it through sporting promotion. This was the case even though this thinking was the basis for a massive funding program for football pools, for government money, and so on.

This had all begun years before at the instigation of the country's former president, Dr. Mannheim. He said that Finland's greatest heritage was its youth, and that the country should develop that youth in sport, culture, and recreation as an investment for future strength and security. I believe he was right, but as it happened his thinking wasn't practically applied.

On my first run at Karhula with Heino's athletes, I first experienced the situation. Along with about twenty-eight of them, I

---

*Paavo Nurmi was an Olympic gold-medalist from Finland who, between 1921 and 1931, set world records in middle- and long-distance events. He is regarded by many experts as the greatest distance runner of the century.

headed out for a 25-kilometer run. It was, admittedly, cold—about 15 degrees below zero—but though I was fifty, I felt quite comfortable as I led these young fellows along. But as we neared the turn, I looked back and saw that there were only two left with me. The other twenty-six had disappeared. I asked my two companions where they were. They shrugged and said they must have gone back home. Sure enough, when we got back, we found the missing twenty-six sitting around comfortably. They'd had their sauna and were drinking coffee. Heino, who was with them, looked at me and said, "Well, there it is. You've seen for yourself."

Maybe he was going to accept it, but I wasn't. I told them they were soft, and, making full use of my limited Finnish, that they had no *sizu*. That's like telling a Finn he has no guts—but that's exactly what I wanted to say. I told them I expected that next time they would run all the way with me.

I later made these same comments to the press. I said that these young men were not hard like their forefathers and that if they wanted to be good runners they would have to get out and train in the winter. The press happily gave it good coverage.

JUOKO KUHA

The best Finnish distance runner of the time was a prime example. Juoko Kuha was a talented young man who, when I met him, didn't really want to have anything to do with me. He was a big star, but, although he was then running around 8 minutes 29 seconds for the steeplechase, he was far from being among the best in the world. Yet the Finns were fêting him as the great runner they had been seeking. They ran his picture on the covers of magazines, and acted as if he was already the great Olympic champion. It was wishful thinking.

During the Finnish winter, they sent Kuha to places like Majorca, the Canary Islands, or Brazil to train. So he was on a glorious training holiday, and perhaps not running as seriously for his country as he was for himself. Kuha was a victim of the lavish government sponsorship that exists in so many countries these days, in the belief that this is the solution to sporting achievement. Kuha, I imagine, didn't appreciate my belief that Finns could train better in the winter if they stayed at home instead of gallivanting off to the summer isles.

Though Kuha did set a world record, he never won an Olympic or European championship medal. He was notable for winning against mediocre runners and failing against good ones. He would run poorly against Gaston Roelants, for instance, and then have a very fast time against unknowns. I knew from the start that he wasn't of the caliber the Finns were hoping for.

Kuha criticized my program every chance he had, insisting that it was no good. Since he had the ears of a lot of Finnish sportswriters who didn't know much about running, he inspired a lot of publicity against me. Subsequently, I met many athletes in the club where Kuha trained, and learned that, as I altered the Finnish training programs to my way of thinking, Kuha began practicing what I had advocated.

Adverse publicity is a problem I can do without. It was fortunate that I couldn't read Finnish. Otherwise I might have left Finland early, despite my belief that if you're confident in what you're doing and keep at it you'll succeed.

GETTING THE RUNNERS OUT

As far as winter training in Finland was concerned, it was tough. I had never run in such cold conditions. My first real run was in 10 degrees below, around a lake in Kuortane. I went out in a thin Mexican track suit and, if I'd known the lake ice was 2 feet thick, I'd have taken a shortcut home across it. But I assumed I had to go all the way around. Everyone was most impressed that I ran the distance as fast as I did; they didn't know I had to run that fast just to keep warm. But, because I ran and survived, the Finns gradually began to get out and run, too. In some towns, when I stepped out in 30 degrees below, it was the girls who followed first. When this happened, the guys followed. I didn't care much who got out first—as long as they all did.

As I observed my reactions to the cold, I was surprised to find that I often seemed to handle the cold conditions better than the Finns. My cheeks blistered on long runs until the Finns taught me to slap on occasional handfuls of snow. This was the only part of my body exposed by the clothing I wore—two track suits, gloves, thick socks, a muffler around my mouth, and a woolen hat over my head and ears. The air I exhaled turned to ice on the muffler, but it was no problem. I soon adopted the Finns' outer track suit, a loose suede cloth suit, which kept out the cold air and meant we were running with a cushion of warm air between it and our bodies. We used the zip as a sort of thermostat.

But I proved it was possible to run and train well. Later, I had an ally in a fine cross-country runner, Paivarainta, who won the world cross-country championship in Spain several years ago. He refused to leave Finland to train during the winter and helped me show others who couldn't afford to head for the sunshine that they didn't have to give up training during those vital months. Since he also got good press, he was a good counter to Kuha.

When I arrived in Finland, their conditioning program for that year's summer track season should have been underway. Since it wasn't, I knew I couldn't influence the results at all. Like anyone else with knowledge of middle- and long-distance running, I knew that it would take me 3 years to get anyone to the top. I could only hope to convince the Finns that, since they weren't succeeding with what they were doing, any change would be for the better. If they instituted a proven program and took a long view of it, they would eventually succeed.

Since I had to find a lure to get them out in the snow, I decided to use the New Zealand system of big road relay-race promotions. By organizing relays, I figured that the handful of keen runners in a club could persuade others to join their teams. I tried several health food organizations for sponsorships, but in the end I had to do like most people who need money for sport—I approached a brewery. With its help, we set up a 100-kilometer relay race from a town called Hameenlinna, northwest of Helsinki and west of Lahti. The first time it achieved a reasonable response, but when I returned 3 years later, thousands of people attended and there were hundreds of runners, including teams from other countries. Now it's one of the biggest and most popular races in Finland.

ORGANIZING A MARATHON

I also set up a marathon. Although it had been firmly established in New Zealand that marathon training was the basis of successful middle- and long-distance running, Finland and most other countries didn't bother with this kind of race. In fact, in 1966, I found that runners had to qualify with 2 hours, 40 minutes to get into Finland's national marathon championship. Since this was Finland's only marathon race, to qualify, runners had to race outside the country. I couldn't get the qualifying conditions changed, so once again I had to find a sponsor. I asked the Turku newspaper to back me, but when I told them it would be run in late January or February—the heart of the Finnish winter—they looked at me as if I was straight from the madhouse. Apparently, they decided I was mad enough to be dangerous—and humored me by agreeing to provide the sponsorship.

"But," they asked, "do you have any idea what it will be like then?"

"Sure," I said. "It'll probably be 20 below zero."

"Or even colder," they said. "You'll never get anyone to enter."

I said I not only expected a good entry, but that every runner would pay an entry fee. This really made them laugh. Finns don't pay anything for racing. Entry fees and all costs are met.

"This time," I repeated, "they pay."

We had 6 weeks in which to organize and advertise the race. In that time we got sixty-five entries. I knew one thing those newspapermen didn't. There were a lot of runners who wanted a qualifying time for the national marathon, and if this was their only chance at home, they'd happily pay the fee.

It was 17 degrees below on the day of the marathon, and everyone ran in track suits and other heavy clothing. About fifty-seven finished, and the winner covered the distance, on dry ice and snow, in 2:27. The sponsors were so overwhelmed they produced a special medal, and the race has prospered since as the Arturii (Finnish for Arthur) annual marathon.

READYING FOR MUNICH

Once I got the Finns running and competing in winter, I was assured of success. Wherever you go, anywhere in the world, there are talented athletes waiting to be brought out. Every city, town, and village has potentially great athletes. It's just a question of motivating them, and giving them the right conditioning program for this potential to develop.

Finland had a head start on a lot of countries, since it already had the facilities. Even Tampere, with 170,000 people, where I was headquartered, has 10 cinder tracks and one Grasstex track. Naturally, until I had the new program going, these tracks were where all the runners trained. They dodged their conditioning work in the forests, and went straight into anaerobic repetition training on the tracks, although their oxygen uptake levels were too low to handle it. It was impossible for them to succeed. The more frustrated they got, the more speed work they did; and the more speed work they did, the worse they became.

I couldn't help comparing their facilities with those we had in New Zealand when Snell, Halberg, and company were setting world records. In Auckland we didn't even have a cinder track then. Snell ran his world records on grass or on a smoothed-out speedway track. Now, with the city nearing a million population, Auckland has one synthetic track, laid in 1975.

But New Zealand doesn't have supermen any more than Finland. Before he joined me, Snell wasn't even the fastest at his high school; and he always remained basically one of the slowest 800-meter runners of the decade. He just had the conditioning to use that basic speed all the way. That, I knew, was all the Finns would need to get back on top.

The Finns succeeded only because they worked with diligence once they had a coordinated program throughout the country. There was no magic to it; they just carried through what I taught them. That's what helped Viren, Vassala, and Kantonen become champions. Not only did they and their coaches have talent and dedication, they were backed by what I think is the best athletic organization in the world.

I was back in Finland in 1970 and predicted then that Munich would be the Finns' Olympics in middle- and long-distance running. I could see the results of their interest in conditioning coming through. I knew that if they continued and went into the vital track season with that conditioning behind them, it wouldn't matter too much what speed work they did. That prediction came true 2 years later.

There was an interesting sidelight to all this and particularly to the Finnish organization in Munich. The Finnish, Swedish, and Norwegian teams were sitting together near the end of the Olympics and the Swedish manager said to the Finnish manager: "How is it you're so successful? Our three teams are much the same in size and yet neither ours nor the Norwegian team have been successful."

The Finnish manager, Mr. Unilla, smiled and replied: "It's interesting that you should make this comment. We have the same number of runners as you and the same number of officials. But there is a difference. Your teams have eight officials—seven managers and one coach. Our team has eight officials—seven coaches and one manager."

There is a lesson to be learned from this—and it's something I had to teach even the Finns when I first went to work with them. They, too, had to be told that the coaches are the important people. Coaches are the ones who teach, motivate, and have the knowledge to develop the great champions.

Until great champions came from their efforts, the Finns had to struggle to make their athletic meetings financially successful. Even though it was receiving plenty of money from the government, the sport was not on a very sound basis.

I had already seen the same problems in New Zealand. It was perhaps worse there because there was no government support. But once Halberg, Snell, and other runners emerged as world champions, the financial situation changed dramatically because they became public drawing cards. Athletic meetings that might earlier have attracted a handful of stalwarts suddenly brought in thousands. This shift in popularity had nothing to do with the administrators. It was entirely due to the athletes and their coaches.

Administrators don't really help the athletes at all. Coaches can do the administrative job just as well, or even better. They know enough about their sport, apart from coaching athletes, to arrange facilities and itineraries, make the contacts to ensure return visits, and obtain the best conditions for their runners. In fact, they can do that aspect of touring better, since they understand the needs of runners.

By the time they reached Munich, the Finnish coaches had control of the racing program—something they didn't have when I first arrived there. Before that, athletes went straight to the officials for anything they needed, but it wasn't always for the best. A lot of money was spent, but training and racing programs were virtually uncontrolled.

I was delighted to see the Finns succeed in Munich.[*] I'd been back several times to check on the programs I had initiated and to

*After Munich, Arthur Lydiard was presented with Finland's highest civilian honor by President Kekonen in recognition of his part in the Munich victories. As well, Lydiard was made a life member of the Finnish A. A. Federation and the National Coaches Association.—G.G.

talk with them about the direction the programs were taking. I knew it was the right direction, so I felt part of their eventual triumph.

One of the initial problems I encountered in Finland was that the physiologists were influencing much of the athletic program. They were certainly advising the coaches. They, in turn, were influenced by Swedish physiologists, who were not right about many of the things they were saying. For example, they advised mixing aerobic and anaerobic training for conditioning, with which I disagree. Psychologically, I feel it's wrong.

It was difficult for me, as a layman, to argue with them. Though I could state my point of view, they did not recognize me as a qualified expert. It didn't impress the Finnish physiologists that, after I had visited the Leipzig sports medicine institute in 1965, the East Germans set up their "Run For Your Life" program based on our book of that name; or that the program had enabled them to double the membership of nearly all their sporting and recreational clubs; or that Jurgen May, the first East German to train with my program, had become a world record-holder.

However, I knew I had enough knowledge to be on strong ground, so I went directly to the administrators and asked them if they were happy with what the physiologists were doing. They replied that they were spending a lot of money, but they were dissatisfied with the results. So I asked to use a telephone so I could invite an East German expert to Finland to explain that the physiologists were wrong and that I was right.

"You'll never get him," they said.

"Watch me," I said. I called Dr. Schuster, head of East German physical education, and explained my problem.

"Certainly," he said. "You can have one of my doctors. How soon do you want him?"

"The sooner the better."

"Will Monday do?" Dr. Schuster asked. "And how long would you like him?"

"Monday will be fine and I'd like him here for two weeks."

Monday saw Dr. Reiss arrive in Finland for a fortnight of lectures and discussions. He succeeded in making the Finns realize that what I was saying was fundamentally correct physiologically, and that they should change their approach.

I was grateful to the East Germans for their cooperation and assistance. Recently, at a conference in India, I pointed out to an East German field events coach that the East Germans were largely responsible for the Finns winning the middle-distance medals in Munich, because they had lifted me over the last hurdle in instituting the necessary changes. It may have required carrying international sporting cooperation further than anyone had intended, but that's what happened.

Chapter 18

Denmark, Russia, and Venezuela

COACHING IN DENMARK

In 1960, after my first Finnish appointment ended, I went first to Germany to lecture and then to Denmark to take in a seminar. This was my first association with the Danes, but I was later invited back to help before Munich. I returned 9 months before the Olympics. The Danes were lax in their training and didn't seem concerned whether they finished first or last. The Finns, on the other hand, had a national feeling about being good runners and took defeat quite bitterly.

The Danes invariably entered races with an inferiority complex. If there were German, Finnish, or British runners in the race, they'd automatically expect defeat. It was difficult to jolt this apathy out of them and get them to train hard. They had never done any distance conditioning and there was no winter program or cross-country season to encourage them.

I had to organize something to trigger them off, which wasn't easy. The Finns had the organization and plenty of money, but there was little cash for sport in Denmark. I soon found that the big business firms didn't really give money for sports promotions. However, this time the Texaco Oil Company came to my rescue, paying my expenses and salary for two 3-month periods so that I could afford to stay there. I really wanted to help the Danes, because I soon found that there were genuine people in Danish athletics, the potential was there, and it is always rewarding to produce something good when the odds are against you.

In November 1971 I settled at Aarhus, on Jutland, where there is a fine tartan (synthetic) track in a forest setting, and some of the best and most beautiful facilities you'll find anywhere in the world. Some of the athletes there were very talented. One was Tom Hansen, who'd run a 3:41 in the 1,500 meters 2 years earlier. But he had been training on interval work ever since, and was getting progressively slower instead of faster. When I got there, he was back to 3:45.

I had to get these runners to realize they had the wrong approach to training. But the first time I called them out for morning training only half of them turned up. Since Tom Hansen was among those who stayed away, I made some caustic remarks to the press that Hansen was haughty in thinking he was so good he didn't have to train in the mornings when Kip Keino and the others considered it vital. The next morning and from then on Hansen trained every day.

Hansen took to marathon training well, and began an immediate improvement. I didn't expect quick results, and told the Danish authorities they would be lucky if I could get one man into a middle-distance final in Munich in the short time available. Just do that, they said, and we'll be happy. They were most cooperative and seemed to understand the problem well.

Near the end of my first 3 months, I took twenty-six Danes to a marathon in West Germany, about 4 hours away. None of them had raced a marathon before. I told them this one was purely for the experience, and that I didn't care where they finished, as long as they did. If you go slow enough, I told them, you'll finish the distance, and that's all I want. It was a cold day, 2 degrees below freezing with a chill wind sweeping down from the North Sea. Not only did they all finish, one of them won the race in 2:23. This was their initiation into the program, and they were as delighted as I was.

I left them with their program, and returned 3 months before the Olympics to get them into their final preparation. They hadn't let me down. Hansen and Gert Larsen made the semifinals of the 1,500, and Hansen ran in the final. He ran last in that, but this didn't surprise me, since, with his limited conditioning, he was so tired at the end of the first two races he could hardly move his legs. One of the Danish women, who I didn't train directly, ran in the semifinals of the 800 meters, which made the Danes ecstatic. They were beginning to look like runners again.

And it's only a matter of time and attention to the program before they will be a force to be reckoned with. Although they lack money and need professional coaches to stimulate interest and coordinate their efforts, they're talented and extremely methodical and businesslike. Once they begin to think seriously enough about it, they'll succeed as athletes and administrators.

I am certain that Hansen, had he not suffered a back injury from which he could not recover in time, would have come close to winning the 1,500 meters in Montreal, particularly in view of the slow pace it followed. He would have been able to follow easily right through to the finishing straight and then kick home, because he had the stamina to match the others and greater basic speed to outsprint them, particularly over the last 50 meters.

At home, the Danes' new program also brought them their first international competition win in many years. Their middle- and long-distance runners beat runners from the Netherlands and Ireland in match racing, so 1972 was a memorable year for them. I don't doubt that, eventually, they will follow the Finns and go right to the top.

Reaching the coaches on these projects isn't always easy, and Denmark was no exception. To get anywhere, I have to deal with the head coaches, the men who attend the Olympics and internationals and set up national programs. It is natural for them to become a little upset when an outsider comes along and tells them what they should be doing. Often my difficulty has been that I haven't had time on my side. I have to try persuasion and, if this isn't going to work, I have to be ruthless. My task is not made any easier by the fact that I'm telling them they must work like hell for at least 3 years before they can expect to see results. It helps, of course, when runners like Hansen and Larsen suddenly move up, but at the start I don't have much to offer except promises.

In Denmark, for instance, the Copenhagen coaches weren't too cooperative. They didn't support my program or help to have it established. The press came to my aid here, with caustic articles questioning why Denmark's most successful athletes were coming from Jutland, while the Copenhagen runners weren't getting anywhere. This put the Copenhagen coaches on the spot, and on my last visit there I got full cooperation from everyone. But it did mean that one section of the country was dragging a little behind the others.

TRAINING IN RUSSIA

While I was in Finland earlier, I had been invited to the Soviet Union. I had said I couldn't go unless I took some Finnish athletes with me. Eventually I was asked to take some cross-country runners to train in Kislovodsk, in the Caucasus. This was a wonderful experience among kind and friendly people, who make visitors feel welcome. We trained hard down there, but, unfortunately, conditions weren't as good as they were in Finland. When the temperature is well below freezing, as it is in Finland, you can run comfortably on snow. But when it is around 32° F as in Kislovodsk, the snow turns slushy. So in spite of the local hospitality, I was forced to take my runners back home.

However, while I was in Russia, I was invited to speak to the Russian coaches. I could tell their head coach wasn't too happy about it, since he didn't agree with my ideas. So I soft-pedalled a bit and didn't press my views too hard, although I've always thought the Soviet Union should do much better than it does in middle- and long-distance running.

Although they might not have wanted my opinions, the Russians were warm and friendly, and willing to exchange views on an informal basis. This happens wherever coaches gather. There is rivalry and differences of opinion, but it doesn't interfere with amicable discussions. It's when you speak on an official, formal basis that you have to watch your tongue a little more carefully.

Later, at a Europe Cup meeting in Sweden, the Russians—who were attending without their head coach—approached me through Khorobkov to talk to them on high-altitude training and other aspects of coaching. This confirmed my feeling that it was coaching leadership that was holding the Russians back.

COACHING IN VENEZUELA

It was a different story altogether in Mexico and Venezuela. I spent 8 months in Mexico in 1966, 8 months in Venezuela in 1970-71, as well as a further 3 months in 1975.

As I mentioned earlier, after Mexico I swore I would never go to another Latin American country. But I weakened and went to Venezuela. Their officials were helpful to a degree, but it again seemed impossible to get a program going. There was plenty of money available, and much latent talent, but the problem was training.

I was working with two runners, Henrico, who was fifteen, and Hernandez, who was sixteen, for 4 months, training for the 1,500 meters. They were skinny youths who looked as if they'd never had a square meal. But they possessed the fantastic qualities I sensed in scores of Venezuelans. At the end of those 4 months, Henrico ran 4:01 for the 1,500 and Hernandez ran 3:57. Another sixteen-year-old was running 400s in 45 to 46 seconds. The possibilities were vast and these kids worked hard. But the political machinery was so counterproductive that those kids may never develop to their world-class potential. The money was channelled the wrong way, and I couldn't get what I needed to finish my program.

There has been a change of government since and perhaps there will be a better approach, but I doubt it. Venezuela is a wealthy country. But the politicians were doing the spending for sport. Invariably, it was more in their own political interests than in the best interests of the country's youth.

Some of the racing in Venezuela was enough to turn a coach's hair grey, if it wasn't already. I recall one marathon that carried on into the night. When the third-place finisher was announced, I heard my runners mumbling to themselves. When I asked them what the trouble was, they told me they had passed this very talented runner, and couldn't understand how he got back up to finish third without passing them. We concluded that, in the cover of darkness, the runner's coach had picked him up and driven him up to the front of the field.

Another race, held in Caracas, featured two fine runners from San Cristobal, which is 7,000 feet up in the Andes. They didn't know the route, but they were out in front and well clear of the field halfway through. I was cruising back and forth on a motorbike watching the race, mainly watching another runner. But the next time I rode up to see how the leaders were doing, the two from San Cristobal were no longer leading. The local coach's two athletes were in front. I found out that he'd turned the San Cristobal boys down the wrong route to let his own men get clear of the field. This was just another problem I was up against. Like the other problems, there was very little I could do about it, except maybe admire the cunning and ingenuity.

I recall the first time I went for training at the *Parque del Este* in Caracas with the Venezuelan sprint coach, Lloyd Murad, who is now living in New Zealand. We told our runners that we expected them to run an easy fartlek session for an hour and meet us at the bus outside the park gates. The *Parque del Este* is one of the most beautiful parks in the world and a fine place for us to train, as there are few areas in Caracas satisfactory for long-distance training.

However, I didn't know that there was a law in Caracas requiring men to wear jackets in the business section of the city. A man who ran about the city or in the parks in shorts was likely to be jeered, catcalled, or worse. Anyway, when the hour had gone and only three runners out of the twenty returned to the bus, I asked Murad if he had given the right directions to the runners. He assured me he had, so we set out to see what had happened.

We found the missing runners guarded by Alsatian dogs in a police compound. Their offense: running in the park in shorts. I thought: "How am I ever going to train these guys?" It took several phone calls to the secretary of the president of Venezuela to secure their release and, later, permission to train in the park in shorts.

The first time I went to San Cristobal, with two coaches and ten athletes, we stayed in a beautiful motel area with gardens and lovely trees. I had a good night's sleep, but when I woke up in the morning I was the only one there. I had no idea where the athletes and coaches were. About 10:30 or 11:00 they started arriving back.

"Where have you been?" I asked. "Did you get up a bit early?"

"Oh, no," was the answer, "we've been over to Cucuta."

Cucuta was about 20 kilometers away, over the border in Colombia.

"What did you go over there for?"

"Ah," they said, "the girls over there are very beautiful and cheap, so we spent the night over there."

It can't have done them much harm, since they ran pretty well in their road race that day, but for a while I thought I had lost my whole team.

In those countries the brothels are more or less legal, and the men go to them quite a lot. In fact, in San Cristobal on the weekends, you don't see many men around.

In another Andes town, Meridas, about 7,000 feet up, we ran several kilometers through deep ravines, as the road winded and twisted high around the hills. There was one particularly sharp bend in the road with a sheer drop away from the edge. There was no fence, but there were thirty or forty little crosses with flowers on the road edge.

I asked my companion, "What happened here? Did a bus go over?"

"No," he laughed. "The men leave town and go down the road to the brothel area, drink, and carry on. Then they come back and drive clean over the cliff."

The mass of crosses perched on the cliff edge looked rather pathetic, but I had to see the funny side of it.

But, that attitude apart, it wasn't difficult to motivate these people into sport. However, obtaining the right facilities and the time to develop the potential were different stories. Many of the officials and politicians who told athletes what to do knew little about athletics or human nature.

This was brought home to me in a little town called Tucapita, near the mouth of the Orinoco River. I took about six runners out early one Sunday morning, heading out along a road that speared straight into the thick jungle. We ran nearly three-quarters of an hour in the hot sun, and by the time we got back our numbers had increased to thirty. Girls and boys of all ages, in bare feet, sandals, and shoes had joined our run for the sheer fun of it.

I noticed that whenever we held a marathon in Venezuela, many kids would accompany the athletes for miles. There was wonderful material there, if I could only have found a way to organize the administrators to harness it. But, after two visits there, it seemed impossible.

Chapter 19

East Germany and the United States

RUNNING IN EAST GERMANY

My first association with the East Germans was through Jurgen May, their first world record-holder. I met him after he had won a 1,500-meter race in Prague in 1965. He told me he had been training on my schedule that year after previously using interval training, as advised by Gershler and Riendell. His old coach had died. He had read *Run To The Top*, and had decided to follow the schedules in it. Jurgen asked me if I would like to visit the Leipzig Sports Medicine Institute. I accepted, and for 2 days discussed training with East German coaches and physiologists. I was impressed by the people I met, and with their open-minded approach to training and exercise physiology generally. Here, many of the best East Germans in these fields were involved in improving athletic standards, as well as the health of the entire nation.

I could see that with their approach they would succeed and become a nation to be reckoned with in any sports they chose. On my return to New Zealand, I made the prediction that in the coming decade East Germany would become one of the world's greatest sporting nations.

Today, they are. Their medals at the Montreal Olympics exceeded even the United States, which had 200 million people against their 18 million. Only the vast Soviet Union defeated them.

In Leipzig, I found that they were interested in what I did with joggers as well as runners. So I presented their head professor, Dr. Schuster, with a copy of *Run For Your Life*, the first book on jogging, which Garth Gilmour and I had just written. Soon after I left, the East Germans set up what they called the "Run For Your Life" national health program. Within six months, this had doubled membership in sporting clubs in the country. They assembled some of their best doctors, physiologists, coaches, sportsmen, and administrators, and mounted a television program designed to interest their people in looking after their own physical welfare. It worked.

After the 1976 Montreal Olympics, I was astounded and dismayed at comments and articles in the press suggesting the East Germans were developing a class of Amazons, were taking dope, and so on. I wonder at the intelligence and ethics of people who say and write such trash without knowing what they are talking about. The East Germans excel in sport because they are more scientific and meticulous than others in what they do. Those who are jealous should take heed that if they, too, do not become more scientific, their country's athletic standards will be even further behind in the next Olympics. Those who are scientific and organized will always beat the unscientific and disorganized.

East German coaches can be found in international coaching clinics throughout the world, trying to assist other nations to improve their standards. Many foreign students are studying in Leipzig so they can take improved sporting development methods back to their own countries. Knowing this, I find it hard to understand the bitterness of some people; it can only be sour grapes.

TRAINING IN THE UNITED STATES

To work and talk with American coaches, too, is a rewarding experience. Most of them have open minds, want to understand different viewpoints, and are eager to learn things to help them become better coaches. The Americans share with the Germans a common thirst for knowledge that will improve the overall standard of sport.

This is a great asset when you begin discussing middle- and long-distance running. There is still much to be learned about arranging balanced programs, evaluating exercises scientifically, and understanding potential development and the limits of human endurance.

Some American athletes and coaches used to reason that they had special problems: long hours of work and study, and the need to peak performance three times a year for the three racing seasons of cross-country, indoor track, and outdoor track. I have yet to find a country where a similar problem does not exist. The answer is the same all over the world: try even harder. And it's happening; young people are going beyond the mental barrier of training over long mileages. Before long, there will be sub-four-minute milers everywhere in the United States.

Americans are discovering that well-conditioned athletes can maintain top form for months, as long as they take simple precautions. These include avoiding training and racing hard at the same time and allowing for recovery from races. Since it's only a matter of keeping fresh and sharp, I see no real problem associated with the three racing seasons. Young Americans who now work hard at conditioning themselves June through early September, and then use anaerobic training in a proper balance, no longer have any problem either.

One problem associated with coaching in America was that coaches were not explaining to athletes why they were carrying out some exercises. When athletes don't understand the objective, they don't work as willingly as they could. I have been out with Americans on training runs and seen them take shortcuts back because they didn't understand the physiological and mechanical aims of the workout. Successful training is intelligent training; intelligent training is knowing the *why* of an exercise, as well as *what* and *how*.

Possibly the main trouble in America was misunderstanding of the value of anaerobic training, which is used excessively in both intensity and volume, even in high schools. Because of this, as well as the tragic lack of organized clubs for young runners when they leave college, the potentially best runners in the country may not become great later on.

Americans need to foster the sport outside of the schools and colleges. Many young Americans have expressed their concern that when they leave college they would be going to areas where there are no clubs and little likelihood of there ever being any. They felt their chances of going any further athletically were remote.

Between 1962 and 1965 there was great depth in middle-distance running in the United States. There were five milers under 3:57, three more under 3:58, and many others under 4:00. Then, the depth diminished and mile running became less strong than it was.

Unquestionably, this is because of the excessive use of anaerobic training. Just when the coaches seemed to be breaking away from the old German interval system, they drifted back to it. Today, however, they seem to be achieving a better balance of training and results.

American coaches have the problem that they must try to recruit athletes for their teams. Valuable coaching time is lost while coaches try to win high-school athletes with scholarship offers, free schooling proposals, and so on. I've seen youngsters of quite mediocre talents treated like Olympic champions, simply to encourage them to attend a particular college and run for its team. The athletes love this but, invariably, the coaches lose control of these runners before they even begin to work with them. Though some schools have plenty of money for recruiting and get the best from the high schools, the results are often poor. College recruiting could be considered a blight on the sport in the United States. But it will be difficult to eradicate or lessen its importance as long as the belief exists that money can buy success.

Appendix

Training Schedules

In addition to the schedules that follow, it is wise to run as many kilometers as possible at easy aerobic efforts. This will help you maintain good general condition, improve your endurance, and assist in recovery from the previous training sessions. Even an extra 15 minutes spent jogging has value.

Regular exercise running on hills will help you in developing and maintaining your speed. Try to fit in some hill springing—uphill running with a driving action—using the ankles and lifting the knees high. Also do some steep hill or step running with high knee lift. Do these whenever you can.

The schedules are only for guidance, to give a balanced method of training for specific events. Always study your reactions to training from day to day, and allow for recovery if you feel jaded or suffer from soreness.

Never do speed training when your muscles are sore, or when you are feeling very tired. Just jog easily, irrespective of what is on the schedule for that day's training. Jogging won't do you any harm, and it will usually assist in overcoming soreness or tiredness. Fast training can lead to injury and add to fatigue. Try to control your training so that you race only when full efforts are required. Run strongly and as easily in effort as possible, always keeping something in reserve. Gradually increase your training tempo as you feel improvement.

Attempt to understand why you are doing your training, and what physiological and mechanical improvement each phase will bring you.

The heading "for as long as possible" on the schedules refers to the period between the finish of the cross-country or road racing season and the start of the specialized track preparation training.

Sprint Events

Weekly training for sprinters should incorporate the following:
1. *Aerobic running:* Some aerobic running should be done regularly. Do enough to raise the steady state, and increase endurance sufficiently so you can get through sprint training without tiring. This can be done as separate training sessions or as cooling down runs after other training. Even a 15-minute run can be effective.
2. *Easy fartlek:* This should be done over easy undulating ground. You should stride out, run fast at times, run a few hilly areas, and generally mix in all types of running training. It allows for the gradual increase of the anaerobic capacity to exercise.
3. *Hill springing:* Since ankle flexibility and power is important, you should work on this training all the time. Bouncing up gentle slopes on your toes will gradually develop power and flexion in the ankles. It will also stretch other leg muscles and tendons, eliminating the risk of strains and pulls. White muscle fibers will develop more efficiency.
4. *Running up steep hills:* The upper leg muscles benefit from this exercise. You need well-conditioned quadriceps to produce the good knee-lift necessary for stride length and speed.
5. *Technique training:* Some should be done so that faulty running actions do not develop during conditioning. This involves some high knee-lift, long striding ankle exercise

running, and running-tall training. It should be done at least once a week.

6. *Relaxed striding:* You should always be relaxed during running. A weekly session of striding several times over 150 to 200 meters with a following wind will help.

7. *Exercising:* Suppling and stretching exercises should be done continually, but particularly before fast training. Exercise your whole body this way every day.

8. *Hurdling:* This can often improve sprinting ability. It can also disclose latent hurdling talents. So it is worth spending time on hurdling and hurdling exercises.

100 AND 200 METERS (BOYS AND GIRLS)

For as long as possible:

Monday	Easy fartlek running, hill springing, steep hills or step running, 15 to 30 minutes
Tuesday	High knee-lift exercises, long striding exercises, running-tall exercises, relaxed striding, 4 x 200 meters
Wednesday	Repeat Monday's session
Thursday	Repeat Tuesday's session
Friday	Leg speed, 4–6 x 100 meters
Saturday	2–3 x 400 meters at ¾ effort
Sunday	Easy fartlek running, 15 to 30 minutes

For 6 weeks:

Monday	Easy fartlek running, hill springing, and steep hills or step running, 15 to 30 minutes
Tuesday	High knee-lift exercises, long-striding exercises, running-tall exercises, relaxed striding, 2 each x 80 meters
Wednesday	Relaxed striding, 4–6 x 200 meters
Thursday	Sprints starts, 4 x 30 meters; fast relaxed running, 4 x 100 meters
Friday	Leg speed, 4–6 x 100 meters
Saturday	Time trials, 100 and 200 meters, or 400 meters
Sunday	Easy fartlek running, 20 to 40 minutes

For 4 weeks:

Monday	2 x 200 meters or 1 x 300 meters, fast
Tuesday	Sprints starts, sprint training, calisthenics
Wednesday	Time trials, 100 and 200 meters, or 400 meters
Thursday	8–12 x 45 meter wind sprints (one every 100 meters)
Friday	Jogging, 15 to 20 minutes
Saturday	Race, 100 and 200 meters, or 400 meters
Sunday	Easy fartlek running, 20 to 40 minutes

For 4 weeks:

Monday	8–12 x 45-meter wind sprints (one every 100 meters)
Tuesday	Fast relaxed running, 4 x 100 meters; sprints starts, 6 x 30 meters

Wednesday	Time trials, 2 x 100 meters and 200 meters
Thursday	Sprint training, calisthenics
Friday	Jogging, 15 to 20 minutes
Saturday	Race
Sunday	Jogging, 20 to 30 minutes

For 1 week:

Monday	Time trials, 1 x 300 meters
Tuesday	Fast relaxed running, 4 x 100 meters
Wednesday	Race, 2 x 100 meters and 200 meters
Thursday	Sprint training, calisthenics
Friday	Jogging, 20 minutes
Saturday	Race, 100 and 200 meters
Sunday	Jogging, 20 to 30 minutes

For 1 week:

Monday	Sprint training, calisthenics
Tuesday	Easy fartlek running, 15 to 20 minutes
Wednesday	Time trials, 2 x 100 meters
Thursday	Relaxed striding, 2 x 200 meters
Friday	Jogging, 15 minutes; or rest
Saturday	First important race
Sunday	Repeat Tuesday's session

Continuation of racing:

Monday	Sprint training, calisthenics
Tuesday	8–12 x 45-meter wind sprints (one every 100 meters)
Wednesday	Race, 100 and 200 meters
Thursday	Easy fartlek running, 15 to 30 minutes
Friday	Relaxed striding, 3–4 x 150 meters; or rest
Saturday	Race
Sunday	Repeat Thursday's session

100 AND 200 METERS (ADULTS)

For as long as possible:

Monday	Easy fartlek running, hill springing, steep hills or step running, ½ hour
Tuesday	High knee-lift exercises, long striding exercises, running-tall exercises, relaxed striding, 4 x 300 meters
Wednesday	Repeat Monday's session
Thursday	Repeat Tuesday's session
Friday	Leg speed, 10 x 120 meters
Saturday	3 x 800 meters at ¾ effort
Sunday	Easy fartlek running, 1 hour

For 6 weeks:

Monday	Easy fartlek running, hill springing, steep hills or step running, ½ hour
Tuesday	High knee-lift exercises, long striding exercises, running-tall exercises, 3 x 100 meters each
Wednesday	Relaxed striding, 8 x 200 meters
Thursday	Sprint starts, 6 x 30 meters; and fast relaxed running, 6 x 100 meters
Friday	Leg speed, 10 x 120 meters
Saturday	Time trials, 100 and 200 meters, or 400 meters
Sunday	Easy fartlek running, 1 hour

For 4 weeks:

Monday	3 x 300 meters or 2 x 500 meters, fast
Tuesday	Sprints starts, sprint training, calisthenics
Wednesday	Time trials, 100 and 200 meters, or 400 meters
Thursday	12—16 x 45 meter wind sprints (one every 100 meters)
Friday	Jogging, ½ hour
Saturday	Race, 100 and 200 meters, or 400 meters
Sunday	Easy fartlek running, ¾ effort

For 4 weeks:

Monday	12 x 45-meter wind sprints (one every 100 meters), or 3 x 300 meters
Tuesday	Fast relaxed running, 6 x 100 meters; and sprint starts, 6 x 30 meters

Wednesday	Time trials, 100 and 200 meters, or 400 meters
Thursday	Sprint training, calisthenics
Friday	Jogging, ½ hour
Saturday	Race
Sunday	Jogging, ¾ hour

For 1 week:

Monday	Time trials, 2 x 500 meters
Tuesday	Fast relaxed running, 6 x 100 meters
Wednesday	Race, 2 x 100 meters, and 200 meters
Thursday	Sprint training, calisthenics
Friday	Jogging, ½ hour
Saturday	Race, 100 and 200 meters, or 400 meters
Sunday	Repeat Friday's session

For 1 week:

Monday	Sprint training, calisthenics
Tuesday	Easy fartlek running, ½ hour
Wednesday	Time trials, 2 x 100 meters
Thursday	Relaxed striding, 3 x 200 meters
Friday	Jogging, ½ hour; or rest
Saturday	Race
Sunday	Jogging, ½ hour

Continuation of racing:

Monday	Calisthenics, sprint starts
Tuesday	Easy fartlek running, ½ to ¾ hour
Wednesday	Time trials, sprints
Thursday	Leg speed, 6–8 x 100 meters
Friday	Rest or jog
Saturday	Race
Sunday	Jogging and relaxed striding, 4–6 x 200 meters

400 METERS (AGES 13–15)

For as long as possible:

Monday	Long aerobic running, 20 to 30 minutes
Tuesday	Long aerobic running, 30 to 45 minutes
Wednesday	Easy fartlek running, 20 to 30 minutes
Thursday	Repeat Tuesday's session
Friday	Relaxed striding, 6 x 150 meters
Saturday	Repeat Tuesday's session
Sunday	Repeat Wednesday's session

For 4 weeks:

Monday	Hill springing, steep hills or step running, ¼ to ½ hour
Tuesday	Long aerobic running, ½ to ¾ hour
Wednesday	Easy fartlek running, 20 to 30 minutes
Thursday	Repeat Tuesday's session
Friday	Repeat Wednesday's session
Saturday	Repeat Monday's session
Sunday	Long aerobic running, ½ to 1 hour

For 4 weeks:

Monday	Hill springing, steep hills or step running, ¼ to ½ hour
Tuesday	Easy fartlek running, ½ to ¾ hour
Wednesday	Leg speed, 6–8 x 100 meters
Thursday	Repeat Tuesday's session
Friday	Repeat Monday's session
Saturday	Repeat Wednesday's session
Sunday	Jogging, ½ to ¾ hour

For 4 weeks:

Monday	Repetitions, 6–10 x 200 meters
Tuesday	8 x sprint training, calisthenics, sprint starts
Wednesday	Easy fartlek running, ½ to ¾ hour
Thursday	Repetitions, 6–10 x 150 meters
Friday	Repeat Tuesday's session
Saturday	Relaxed striding, 4 x 300 meters
Sunday	Jogging, ½ to 1 hour

For 2 weeks:

Monday	2 x 300 meters (15-minute interval)
Tuesday	8 x sprint training, calisthenics, sprint starts
Wednesday	Time trials, 100, 300 and 600 meters
Thursday	Easy fartlek running, ½ hour
Friday	Fast relaxed running, 6 x 100 meters
Saturday	Time trials, 2 x 800 meters
Sunday	Jogging, ½ to 1 hour

For 2 weeks:

Monday	6–8 x 45-meter wind sprints (one every 200 meters)
Tuesday	6 x sprint training, calisthenics, sprint starts
Wednesday	Race, 100 and 400 meters
Thursday	Easy fartlek running, ½ hour
Friday	Relaxed striding, 4 x 200 meters
Saturday	Race, 200 and 400 meters
Sunday	Jogging, ½ hour

For 1 week:

Monday	8–10 x 45-meter wind sprints (one every 100 meters)
Tuesday	6 x sprint training, calisthenics, sprint starts
Wednesday	Race, 400 meters
Thursday	Easy fartlek running, ½ hour
Friday	Relaxed striding, 2 x 300 meters
Saturday	Race, 100 and 200 meters
Sunday	Jogging, ½ hour

For 1 week:

Monday	6–8 x 45-meter wind sprints (one every 100 meters)
Tuesday	Easy fartlek running, ½ hour
Wednesday	Race, 100 and 200 meters
Thursday	Jogging, ½ hour
Friday	Jogging, ½ hour; or rest
Saturday	First important race
Sunday	Jogging, ½ hour

Continuation of racing:

Monday	8–10 x 45-meter wind sprints (one every 100 meters)
Tuesday	6–8 x sprint training, calisthenics, sprints starts

Wednesday	Race
Thursday	Easy fartlek running, ½ hour
Friday	Relaxed striding, 3 x 200 meters
Saturday	Race
Sunday	Jogging, ½ to ¾ hour

400 METERS (AGES 16–18)

For as long as possible:

Monday	Long aerobic running, ½ to ¾ hour
Tuesday	Long aerobic running, ¾ to 1 hour
Wednesday	Easy fartlek running, ½ to ¾ hour
Thursday	Repeat Tuesday's session
Friday	Relaxed striding, 6 x 200 meters
Saturday	Long aerobic running, ¾ to 1¼ hours
Sunday	Easy fartlek running, ½ to 1 hour

For 2 weeks:

Monday	Hill springing, steep hills or step running, ½ to ¾ hour
Tuesday	Long aerobic running, ¾ to 1 hour
Wednesday	Easy fartlek running, ¾ to 1 hour
Thursday	Repeat Tuesday's session
Friday	Easy fartlek running, ½ hour
Saturday	Hill springing, steep hills or step running, ½ to ¾ hours
Sunday	Long aerobic running, ¾ to 1¼ hours

For 2 weeks:

Monday	Hill springing, steep hills or step running, ½ to ¾ hour
Tuesday	Easy fartlek running, ¾ to 1 hour
Wednesday	Leg speed, 8 x 100 meters
Thursday	Repeat Tuesday's session
Friday	Repeat Monday's session
Saturday	Leg speed, 8–10 x 100 meters
Sunday	Jogging, 1 hour

For 4 weeks:

Monday	Repetitions, 8–12 x 200 meters
Tuesday	8–10 x sprint training, calisthenics, sprints starts
Wednesday	Easy fartlek running, ¾ to I hour
Thursday	Repetitions, 6–8 x 400 meters
Friday	Repeat Tuesday's session
Saturday	Relaxed striding, 6 x 300 meters
Sunday	Jogging, 1 hour

For 2 weeks:

Monday	3 x 300 meters; or 2 x 500 meters
Tuesday	10 x sprint training, calisthenics, sprints starts
Wednesday	Time trials, 100, 300 and 600 meters
Thursday	Easy fartlek running, ¾ hour
Friday	Fast relaxed running, 6 x 120 meters
Saturday	Time trials, 3 x 800 meters
Sunday	Jogging, 1 hour

For 2 weeks:

Monday	8–10 x 100-meter wind sprints (one every 200 meters)
Tuesday	8 x sprint training, calisthenics, sprints starts
Wednesday	Race, 100 and 400 meters
Thursday	Easy fartlek running, ¾ hour
Friday	Relaxed striding, 6 x 200 meters
Saturday	Race, 200 and 400 meters
Sunday	Jogging, ¾ hour

For 1 week:

Monday	12 x 45-meter wind sprints (one every 100 meters)
Tuesday	8 x sprint training, calisthenics, sprints starts
Wednesday	Race, 400 meters
Thursday	Easy fartlek running, ¾ hour
Friday	Relaxed striding, 3 x 300 meters
Saturday	Race, 100 and 200 meters
Sunday	Jogging, ¾ hour

For 1 week:

Monday	12 x 45-meter wind sprints (one every 100 meters)
Tuesday	Easy fartlek running, ½ to ¾ hour
Wednesday	Race, 2 x 200 meters
Thursday	Jogging, ½ to ¾ hour
Friday	Jogging, ½ hour; or rest
Saturday	First important race
Sunday	Jogging, ¾ hour

Continuation of racing:

Monday	12 x 45-meter wind sprints (one every 100 meters)

Tuesday	8 x sprint training, calisthenics, sprints starts
Wednesday	Race
Thursday	Easy fartlek running, ½ to ¾ hour
Friday	Relaxed striding, 4 x 200 meters
Saturday	Race
Sunday	Jogging, ¾ to 1 hour

400 METERS (ADULTS)

For as long as possible:

Monday	Long aerobic running, ½ hour
Tuesday	Long aerobic running, 1 hour
Wednesday	Easy fartlek running, ¾ to 1 hour
Thursday	Repeat Tuesday's session
Friday	Relaxed striding, 6 x 200 meters
Saturday	Long aerobic running, 1 to 1½ hours
Sunday	Repeat Wednesday's session

For 2 weeks:

Monday	Hill springing, steep hills or step running, ¾ hour
Tuesday	Long aerobic running, 1 hour
Wednesday	Easy fartlek running, 1 hour
Thursday	Repeat Tuesday's session
Friday	Easy fartlek running, ¾ hour
Saturday	Repeat Monday's session
Sunday	Long aerobic running, 1 to 1½ hours

For 2 weeks:

Monday	Hill springing, steep hills or step running, ¾ hour
Tuesday	Easy fartlek running, 1 hour
Wednesday	Leg speed, 10 x 100 meters
Thursday	Repeat Tuesday's session
Friday	Repeat Monday's session
Saturday	Repeat Wednesday's session
Sunday	Jogging, 1 hour

For 4 weeks:

Monday	Repetitions, 10–12 x 200 meters
Tuesday	10 x sprint training, calisthenics, sprints starts
Wednesday	Easy fartlek running, 1 hour
Thursday	Repetitions, 8 x 400 meters
Friday	Sprint training, calisthenics
Saturday	Relaxed striding, 6 x 300 meters
Sunday	Jogging, 1 hour

For 2 weeks:

Monday	3 x 300 meters; or 2 x 500 meters
Tuesday	10 x sprint training, calisthenics, sprints starts
Wednesday	Time trials, 100, 300 and 600 meters
Thursday	Easy fartlek running, 1 hour
Friday	Fast relaxed running, 6 x 120 meters
Saturday	Time trials, 3 x 800 meters
Sunday	Jogging, 1 hour

For 2 weeks:

Monday	10 x 100-meter wind sprints (one every 200 meters)
Tuesday	10 x sprint training, calisthenics, sprints starts
Wednesday	Race, 100 and 400 meters
Thursday	Easy fartlek running, 1 hour
Friday	Relaxed striding, 6 x 200 meters
Saturday	Race, 200 and 400 meters
Sunday	Jogging, 1 hour

For 1 week:

Monday	16 x 45-meter wind sprints (one every 100 meters)
Tuesday	10 x sprint training, calisthenics, sprints starts
Wednesday	Race, 2 x 400 meters
Thursday	Easy fartlek running, 1 hour
Friday	Relaxed striding, 3 x 300 meters
Saturday	Race, 100 and 200 meters
Sunday	Jogging, ¾ hour

For 1 week:

Monday	12 x 45-meter wind sprints (one every 100 meters)
Tuesday	Easy fartlek running, ¾ hour
Wednesday	Race, 2 x 200 meters
Thursday	Jogging, ¾ hour
Friday	Jogging, 1 hour; or rest
Saturday	First important race
Sunday	Jogging, 1 hour

Continuation of racing:

Monday	12 x 45-meter wind sprints (one every 100 meters)
Tuesday	10 x sprint training, calisthenics, sprints starts

Wednesday	Race
Thursday	Easy fartlek running, ¾ to 1 hour
Friday	Relaxed striding, 4 x 200 meters
Saturday	Race
Sunday	Jogging, 1 hour

Track Distances

800 AND 1,500 METERS (AGES 10-12)

For as long as possible:

Monday	Long aerobic running, ¼ to ½ hour
Tuesday	Long aerobic running, ¼ to ¾ hour
Wednesday	Time trials, 2,000 meters
Thursday	Long aerobic running, ½ to ¾ hour
Friday	Easy fartlek running, ¼ to ½ hour
Saturday	Time trials, 3,000 meters
Sunday	Long aerobic running, ½ to 1 hour

For 4 weeks:

Monday	Leg speed, 6 x 60 meters
Tuesday	Long aerobic running, ¼ to ¾ hour
Wednesday	Hill springing, steep hills or step running, ¼ to ½ hour
Thursday	Easy fartlek running, ¼ to ½ hour
Friday	Repeat Monday's session
Saturday	Repeat Wednesday's session
Sunday	Long aerobic running, ½ to 1 hour

For 4 weeks:

Monday	4–6 x 100-meter wind sprints (one every 200 meters)
Tuesday	High knee-lift exercises, long striding exercises, running-tall exercises, 2 x 60 meters
Wednesday	Easy fartlek running, ¼ to ½ hour
Thursday	Repetitions, 2–4 x 150 meters
Friday	Leg speed, 4–6 x 60 meters
Saturday	Time trials, 1,600 meters
Sunday	Long aerobic running, ½ to 1 hour

For 4 weeks:

Monday	4–8 x 45-meter wind sprints (one every 100 meters)
Tuesday	Easy fartlek running, ¼ to ½ hour
Wednesday	Time trials, 100 and 400 meters
Thursday	Long aerobic running, ¼ to ½ hour
Friday	Rest
Saturday	Race, 400 or 800 meters
Sunday	Jogging, ½ to ¾ hour

For 1 week:

Monday	Pace judgment running, 4–8 x 45-meter wind sprints (one every 100 meters)
Tuesday	Easy fartlek running, ¼ hour
Wednesday	Time trials, race distance
Thursday	Repeat Tuesday's session
Friday	Rest
Saturday	Race, 200 or 400 meters
Sunday	Jogging, ½ to 1 hour

For 1 week:

Monday	4–8 x 45-meter wind sprints (one every 100 meters)
Tuesday	Easy fartlek running, ¼ hour
Wednesday	Time trials, 200 meters
Thursday	Jogging, ¼ to ½ hour
Friday	Rest
Saturday	First important race
Sunday	Jogging, ½ to 1 hour

Continuation of racing:

Monday	Easy fartlek running, ¼ to ½ hour
Tuesday	Relaxed striding, 2 x 100 meters
Wednesday	Race or time trials, 200 meters
Thursday	Easy fartlek running, ¼ hour
Friday	Rest
Saturday	Race or time trials, 400 or 800 meters
Sunday	Jogging, ½ to 1 hour

800 AND 1,500 METERS (BOYS, AGES 13-14)

For as long as possible:

Monday	Long aerobic running, ½ to ¾ hour
Tuesday	Long aerobic running, ¾ to 1¼ hour
Wednesday	Time trials, 3,000 meters
Thursday	Long aerobic running, ¼ to 1¼ hours
Friday	Easy fartlek running, ½ hour
Saturday	Time trials, 5,000 meters
Sunday	Long aerobic running, ¾ to 1½ hours

For 4 weeks:

Monday	Leg speed, 6–8 x 80 meters
Tuesday	Long aerobic running, ¾ to 1¼ hours
Wednesday	Hill springing, steep hills or step running, ½ hour
Thursday	Easy fartlek running, ½ to ¾ hour
Friday	Repeat Monday's session
Saturday	Repeat Wednesday's session
Sunday	Repeat Tuesday's session

For 4 weeks:

Monday	Repetitions, 6–10 x 200 meters
Tuesday	High knee-lift exercises, long striding exercises, running-tall exercises, fast relaxed running, 2 x 80 meters
Wednesday	Easy fartlek running, ½ to ¾ hour
Thursday	Repeat Monday's session
Friday	Leg speed, 4–6 x 80 meters
Saturday	Time trials, 3,000 meters
Sunday	Long aerobic running, ¾ to 1¼ hours

For 4 weeks:

Monday	6–8 x 100-meter wind sprints (one every 200 meters)
Tuesday	Easy fartlek running, ½ to ¾ hour
Wednesday	Time trials, 200 and 600 meters
Thursday	Long aerobic running, ½ hour
Friday	Fast relaxed running, 3 x 80 meters
Saturday	Race, 800 or 1,500 meters
Sunday	Jogging, ¼ to 1 hour

For 1 week:

Monday	8–10 x 45-meter wind sprints (one every 100 meters)
Tuesday	Easy fartlek running, ½ hour
Wednesday	Time trials, race distance, pace judgment running, fast
Thursday	Easy fartlek running, ½ to ¾ hour
Friday	Relaxed striding, 3 x 200 meters
Saturday	Race, 400 or 800 meters
Sunday	Jogging, ¾ to 1 hour

For 1 week:

Monday	8 x 45-meter wind sprints (one every 100 meters)
Tuesday	Easy fartlek running, ½ hour
Wednesday	Time trials, 200 meters
Thursday	Jogging, ½ hour
Friday	Jogging, ½ hour; or rest
Saturday	First important race
Sunday	Jogging, ¾ to 1 hour

Continuation of racing:

Monday	Easy fartlek running, ½ hour
Tuesday	Relaxed striding, 3 x 100 meters
Wednesday	Race or time trial, 400 meters
Thursday	Repeat Monday's session
Friday	Repeat Tuesday's session
Saturday	Race or time trials, 400 or 800 meters
Sunday	Jogging, ¾ to 1 hour

800 AND 1,500 METERS (GIRLS, AGES 13–14)

For as long as possible:

Monday	Easy fartlek running, ½ to ¾ hour
Tuesday	Long aerobic running, ½ to 1 hour
Wednesday	Time trials, 2,400 meters
Thursday	Repeat Tuesday's session
Friday	Repeat Monday's session
Saturday	Time trials, 4,000 meters
Sunday	Long aerobic running, ¾ to 1¼ hours

For 4 weeks:

Monday	Leg speed, 6–8 x 80 meters
Tuesday	Long aerobic running, ½ to 1 hour
Wednesday	Hill springing, steep hills or step running, 20 to 30 minutes
Thursday	Easy fartlek running, ½ to ¾ hour
Friday	Repeat Monday's session
Saturday	Repeat Wednesday's session
Sunday	Long aerobic running, ¾ to 1¼ hours

For 4 weeks:

Monday	Repetitions, 4–6 x 200 meters
Tuesday	High knee-lift exercises, long striding exercises, running-tall exercises, 2 x 80 meters; fast relaxed running, 2 x 100 meters
Wednesday	Easy fartlek running, ½ to ¾ hour
Thursday	Repeat Monday's session
Friday	Leg speed, 4–6 x 80 meters
Saturday	Time trials, 2,000 meters
Sunday	Long aerobic running, ¾ to 1¼ hours

For 4 weeks:

Monday	8–12 x 45-meter wind sprints (one every 100 meters)
Tuesday	Easy fartlek running, ½ to ¾ hour
Wednesday	Time trials, 100 and 400 meters
Thursday	Long aerobic running, ½ hour
Friday	Relaxed striding, 3 x 100 meters
Saturday	Race, 400 or 800 meters
Sunday	Jogging, ½ to 1 hour

For 1 week:

Monday	8 x 45-meter wind sprints (one every 100 meters)
Tuesday	Easy fartlek running, 20 to 30 minutes
Wednesday	Time trial, race distance
Thursday	Repeat Tuesday's session
Friday	Relaxed striding, 3 x 100 meters
Saturday	Race, 200 or 400 meters
Sunday	Jogging, ¾ to 1 hour

For 1 week:

Monday	6–8 x 45-meter wind sprints (one every 100 meters)
Tuesday	Easy fartlek running, 20 to 30 minutes
Wednesday	Time trials, 200 meters
Thursday	Jogging, ½ hour
Friday	Jogging, ½ hour; or rest
Saturday	First important race
Sunday	Jogging, ¾ to 1 hour

Continuation of racing:

Monday	Easy fartlek running, 20 to 30 minutes
Tuesday	Relaxed striding, 3 x 100 meters
Wednesday	Race or time trial, 400 meters
Thursday	Repeat Tuesday's session
Friday	Repeat Tuesday's session
Saturday	Race or time trial, 400 or 800 meters
Sunday	Jogging, ½ to ¾ hour

800 AND 1,500 METERS (BOYS, AGES 15-16)

For as long as possible:

Monday	Easy fartlek running, ½ to ¾ hour
Tuesday	Long aerobic running, 1 to 1¼ hours
Wednesday	Time trials, 3,000 meters
Thursday	Repeat Tuesday's session
Friday	Easy fartlek running, ½ hour
Saturday	Time trials, 5,000 meters
Sunday	Long aerobic running, 1 to 1½ hours

For 4 weeks:

Monday	Leg speed, 6–8 x 100 meters
Tuesday	Long aerobic running, 1 to 1¼ hours
Wednesday	Hill springing, steep hills or step running, ½ to ¾ hour
Thursday	Easy fartlek running, ½ to ¾ hour
Friday	Repeat Monday's session
Saturday	Repeat Wednesday's session
Sunday	Long aerobic running, 1 to 1½ hours

For 4 weeks:

Monday	Repetitions, 8–12 x 400 meters
Tuesday	High knee-lift exercises, long striding exercises, running-tall exercises, fast relaxed running, 2 x 100 meters
Wednesday	Easy fartlek running, ½ to ¾ hour
Thursday	Repetitions, 8–12 x 200 meters
Friday	Leg speed, 6 x 100 meters
Saturday	Time trials, 3,000 meters
Sunday	Long aerobic running, 1 to 1½ hours

For 4 weeks:

Monday	6–8 x 100-meter wind sprints (one every 200 meters)
Tuesday	Easy fartlek running, ½ to ¾ hour
Wednesday	Time trials, 200 and 600 meters
Thursday	Jogging, ¾ hour
Friday	Fast relaxed running, 4 x 100 meters
Saturday	Race, 800 or 1,500 meters
Sunday	Jogging, 1 to 1½ hours

For 1 week:

Monday	12 x 45-meter wind sprints (one every 100 meters)
Tuesday	Easy fartlek running, ½ hour
Wednesday	Time trials, race distance
Thursday	Repeat Tuesday's session
Friday	Relaxed striding, 4 x 200 meters
Saturday	Race, 400 meters or 800 meters
Sunday	Jogging, 1 hour

For 1 week:

Monday	8–12 x 45-meter wind sprints (one every 100 meters)
Tuesday	Easy fartlek running, ½ hour
Wednesday	Time trials, 100 and 400 meters
Thursday	Jogging, ¾ hour
Friday	Jogging, ½ hour
Saturday	First important race
Sunday	Jogging, 1 hour or more

Continuation of racing:

Monday	Easy fartlek running, ½ hour
Tuesday	Relaxed striding, 4 x 200 meters
Wednesday	Race or time trials
Thursday	Repeat Monday's sessions
Friday	Repeat Tuesday's session
Saturday	Race or time trials
Sunday	Jogging, 1 hour or more

800 AND 1,500 METERS (GIRLS, AGES 15–17)

For as long as possible:

Monday	Easy fartlek running, ¾ to 1 hour
Tuesday	Long aerobic running, ¾ to 1¼ hour
Wednesday	Time trials, 3,000 meters
Thursday	Repeat Tuesday's session
Friday	Easy fartlek running, ½ to ¾ hour (hills)
Saturday	Time trials, 5,000 meters
Sunday	Long aerobic running, 1 to 1½ hours

For 4 weeks:

Monday	Leg speed, 8–10 x 100 meters
Tuesday	Long aerobic running, ¾ to 1¼ hours
Wednesday	Hill springing, steep hills or step running, ½ to ¾ hours
Thursday	Easy fartlek running, ¾ to 1 hour
Friday	Repeat Monday's session
Saturday	Repeat Wednesday's session
Sunday	Long aerobic running, 1 to 1½ hours

For 4 weeks:

Monday	Repetitions, 8–12 x 200 meters
Tuesday	High knee-lift exercises, long striding exercises, and running-tall exercises, 2 x 200 meters; fast relaxed running, 3 x 100 meters
Wednesday	Easy fartlek running, ¾ to 1 hour
Thursday	Repeat Monday's session
Friday	Leg speed, 6 x 100 meters
Saturday	Time trials, 3,000 meters
Sunday	Long aerobic running, 1 to 1½ hours

For 4 weeks:

Monday	8–10 x 100-meter wind sprints (one every 200 meters)
Tuesday	Easy fartlek running, ¾ to 1 hour
Wednesday	Time trials, 200 and 600 meters
Thursday	Long aerobic running, ¾ hour
Friday	Fast relaxed running, 4 x 100 meters
Saturday	Race, 800 meters or 1,500 meters
Sunday	Jogging, ¾ to 1¼ hours

For 1 week:

Monday	8–12 x 45-meter wind sprints (one every 100 meters)
Tuesday	Easy fartlek running, ½ to ¾ hour
Wednesday	Time trials, race distance
Thursday	Repeat Tuesday's distance
Friday	Relaxed striding, 4 x 200 meters
Saturday	Race, 400 or 800 meters
Sunday	Jogging, ¾ to 1 hour

For 1 week:

Monday	8–12 x 45-meter wind sprints (one every 100 meters)
Tuesday	Easy fartlek running, ¾ hour
Wednesday	Time trials, 100 and 400 meters
Thursday	Jogging, ½ hour
Friday	Repeat Thursday's session
Saturday	First important race
Sunday	Jogging, ¾ to 1¼ hours

Continuation of racing:

Monday	Easy fartlek running, ½ to ¾ hours
Tuesday	Relaxed striding, 4 x 200 meters
Wednesday	Race or 8 x 100-meter wind sprints (one every 200 meters)
Thursday	Repeat Monday's session
Friday	Repeat Tuesday's session
Saturday	Race or time trials, 800 or 1,500 meters
Sunday	Jogging, ¾ to 1 hour

800 AND 1,500 METERS (BOYS, AGES 17–18)

For as long as possible:

Monday	Easy fartlek running, ¾ hour
Tuesday	Long aerobic running, 1 to 1¼ hours
Wednesday	Time trials, 3,000 meters
Thursday	Repeat Tuesday's session
Friday	Easy fartlek running, ½ hour
Saturday	Time trials, 5,000 meters
Sunday	Long aerobic running, 1½ hours or more

For 4 weeks:

Monday	Leg speed, 8–10 x 100 meters
Tuesday	Long aerobic running, 1 to 1¼ hours
Wednesday	Hill springing, steep hills or step running, ¾ hour
Thursday	Easy fartlek running, ¾ hour
Friday	Repeat Monday's session
Saturday	Repeat Wednesday's session
Sunday	Long aerobic running, 1½ hours or more

For 4 weeks:

Monday	Repetitions, 10–15 x 400 meters
Tuesday	High knee-lift exercises, long striding exercises, running-tall exercises, 2 x 100 meters; fast relaxed running, 4 x 100 meters
Wednesday	Easy fartlek running, ¾ hour
Thursday	Repetitions, 10–15 x 200 meters
Friday	Leg speed, 6–8 x 100 meters
Saturday	Time trials, 3,000 meters
Sunday	Long aerobic running, 1½ hours or more

For 4 weeks:

Monday	8-10 x 100-meter wind sprints (one every 200 meters)
Tuesday	Easy fartlek running, ¾ hour
Wednesday	Time trials, 200 and 600 meters
Thursday	Jogging, ¾ hour
Friday	Fast relaxed running, 6 x 100 meters
Saturday	Race, 800 or 1,500 meters
Sunday	Jogging, 1 to 1¼ hours

For 1 week:

Monday	16 x 45-meter wind sprints (one every 100 meters)
Tuesday	Easy fartlek running, ½ hour
Wednesday	Time trials, race distance
Thursday	Easy fartlek running, ¾ hour
Friday	Relaxed striding, 4 x 200 meters
Saturday	Race, 400 or 800 meters
Sunday	Jogging, 1 hour

For 1 week:

Monday	12 x 45-meter wind sprints (one every 100 meters)
Tuesday	Easy fartlek running, ½ hour
Wednesday	Time trials, 100 and 400 meters
Thursday	Jogging, ¾ hour
Friday	Jogging, ½ hour
Saturday	First important race
Sunday	Jogging, 1 hour or more

Continuation of racing:

Monday	Easy fartlek running, ¾ hour
Tuesday	Relaxed striding, 4 x 200 meters
Wednesday	Race or time trials
Thursday	Repeat Monday's session
Friday	Repeat Tuesday's session
Saturday	Race or time trials
Sunday	Jogging, 1 hour or more

800 AND 1,500 METERS (BOYS, AGES 19–20)

For as long as possible:

Monday	Easy fartlek running, ¾ to 1 hour
Tuesday	Long aerobic running, 1 to 1½ hours
Wednesday	Time trials, 5,000 meters
Thursday	Repeat Tuesday's session
Friday	Easy fartlek running, ¾ hour
Saturday	Time trials, 10,000 meters
Sunday	Long aerobic running 1½ to 2 hours

For 4 weeks:

Monday	Leg speed, 10 x 100 meters
Tuesday	Long aerobic running, 1 to 1½ hours
Wednesday	Hill springing, steep hills or step running, ¾ to 1 hour
Thursday	Easy fartlek running, ¾ to 1 hour
Friday	Repeat Monday's session
Saturday	Repeat Wednesday's session
Sunday	Long aerobic running, 1½ to 2 hours

For 4 weeks:

Monday	Repetitions, 12–16 x 400 meters
Tuesday	High knee-lift exercises, long striding exercises, running-tall exercises, 2 x 100 meters; fast relaxed running, 4 x 100 meters
Wednesday	Easy fartlek running, ¾ to 1 hour
Thursday	Repetitions, 15–20 x 200 meters
Friday	Leg speed, 8 x 100 meters
Saturday	Time trials, 3,000 or 5,000 meters
Sunday	Long aerobic running, 1½ to 2 hours

For 4 weeks:

Monday	10–12 x 100-meter wind sprints (one every 200 meters)
Tuesday	Easy fartlek running, ¾ to 1 hour
Wednesday	Time trials, 200 and 600 meters
Thursday	Long aerobic running, ¾ hour
Friday	Fast relaxed running, 6 x 100 meters
Saturday	Race, 800 or 1,500 meters
Sunday	Jogging, 1½ hours

For 1 week:

Monday	16 x 45-meter wind sprints (one every 100 meters)
Tuesday	Easy fartlek running, ¾ hour
Wednesday	Time trials, race distance
Thursday	Repeat Tuesday's session
Friday	Relaxed striding, 4 x 200 meters
Saturday	Race, 400 or 800 meters
Sunday	Jogging, 1½ hours

For 1 week:

Monday	12 x 45-meter wind sprints (one every 100 meters)
Tuesday	Easy fartlek running, ½ hour
Wednesday	Time trials, 100 and 400 meters
Thursday	Jogging, ¾ hour
Friday	Jogging, ½ hour
Saturday	First important race
Sunday	Jogging, 1½ hours

Continuation of racing:

Monday	Easy fartlek running, ¾ hour
Tuesday	Relaxed striding, 4 x 200 meters
Wednesday	Race or time trials
Thursday	Repeat Monday's session
Friday	Repeat Tuesday's session
Saturday	Race or time trials
Sunday	Jogging, 1½ hours

800 AND 1,500 METERS (MEN)

For as long as possible:

Monday	Easy fartlek running, 1 hour
Tuesday	Long aerobic running, 1½ hours
Wednesday	Time trials, 5,000 meters
Thursday	Repeat Tuesday's session
Friday	Easy fartlek running, ¾ hour; and hills
Saturday	Time trials, 10,000 meters
Sunday	Aerobic running, 1½ hours or more

For 4 weeks:

Monday	Leg speed, 10 x 120 meters
Tuesday	Long aerobic running, 1½ hours
Wednesday	Hill springing, steep hills or step running, 1 hour
Thursday	Easy fartlek running, 1 hour
Friday	Repeat Monday's session
Saturday	Repeat Wednesday's session
Sunday	Long aerobic running, 1½ hours or more

For 4 weeks:

Monday	Repetitions, 15–20 x 400 meters
Tuesday	High knee-lift exercises, long striding exercises, running-tall exercises, 2 x 100 meters; fast relaxed running, 4 x 100 meters
Wednesday	Easy fartlek running, 1 hour
Thursday	Repetitions, 15–20 x 200 meters
Friday	Leg speed, 10 x 100 meters
Saturday	Time trials, 3,000 or 5,000 meters
Sunday	Long aerobic running, 1½ hours or more

For 4 weeks:

Monday	12–14 x 100-meter wind sprints (one every 100 meters)
Tuesday	Easy fartlek running, 1 hour
Wednesday	Time trials, 200 and 600 meters
Thursday	Long aerobic running, 1 hour
Friday	Fast relaxed running, 6 x 100 meters
Saturday	Race, 800 or 1,500 meters
Sunday	Jogging, 1½ hours

For 1 week:

Monday	20 x 45-meter wind sprints (one every 100 meters)
Tuesday	Easy fartlek running, 1 hour
Wednesday	Time trials, race distance
Thursday	Easy fartlek running, ¾ hour
Friday	Relaxed striding, 6 x 400 meters
Saturday	Race, 400 or 800 meters
Sunday	Jogging, 1½ hours

For 1 week:

Monday	16 x 45-meter wind sprints (one every 100 meters)
Tuesday	Easy fartlek running, ¾ hour
Wednesday	Time trials, 100 and 400 meters
Thursday	Jogging, ¾ hour
Friday	Jogging, ½ hour
Saturday	First important race
Sunday	Jogging, 1½ hours

Continuation of racing:

Monday	Easy fartlek running, 1 hour
Tuesday	Relaxed striding, 6 x 200 meters
Wednesday	Race or 12 x 100-meter wind sprints (one every 200 meters)
Thursday	Repeat Monday's session
Friday	Repeat Tuesday's session
Saturday	Race or time trials
Sunday	Jogging, 1½ hours

800 AND 1,500 METERS (WOMEN)

For as long as possible:

Monday	Easy fartlek running, ¾ to 1 hour
Tuesday	Long aerobic running, 1 to 1½ hours
Wednesday	Time trials, 3,000 meters
Thursday	Repeat Tuesday's session
Friday	Easy fartlek running, ¾ hour
Saturday	Time trials, 5,000 meters
Sunday	Long aerobic running, 1½ hours or more

For 4 weeks:

Monday	Leg speed, 10 x 100 meters
Tuesday	Long aerobic running, 1 to 1½ hours
Wednesday	Hill springing, steep hills or step running, ¾ to 1 hour
Thursday	Easy fartlek running, ¾ to 1 hour
Friday	Repeat Monday's session
Saturday	Repeat Wednesday's session
Sunday	Long aerobic running, 1½ hours or more

For 4 weeks:

Monday	Repetitions, 10–15 x 400 meters
Tuesday	High knee-lift, long striding exercises, running-tall exercises, 2 x 100 meters; fast relaxed running, 4 x 100 meters
Wednesday	Easy fartlek running, ¾ to 1 hour
Thursday	Repetitions, 12–18 x 200 meters
Friday	Leg speed, 8 x 100 meters
Saturday	Time trials, 3,000 meters
Sunday	Long aerobic running, 1½ hours or more

For 4 weeks:

Monday	8–10 x 100-meter wind sprints (one every 200 meters)
Tuesday	Easy fartlek running, ¾ to 1 hour
Wednesday	Time trials, 200 and 600 meters
Thursday	Long aerobic running, ¾ hour
Friday	Fast relaxed running, 6 x 100 meters
Saturday	Race, 800 or 1,500 meters
Sunday	Jogging, 1 to 1½ hours

For 1 week:

Monday	12–16 x 45-meter wind sprints (one every 100 meters)
Tuesday	Easy fartlek running, ¾ hour
Wednesday	Time trials, race distance
Thursday	Repeat Tuesday's session
Friday	Relaxed striding, 4 x 200 meters
Saturday	Race, 400 or 800 meters
Sunday	Jogging, 1 to 1½ hours

For 1 week:

Monday	12 x 45-meter wind sprints (one every 100 meters)
Tuesday	Easy fartlek running, ¾ hour
Wednesday	Time trials, 100 and 400 meters
Thursday	Jogging, ¾ hour
Friday	Jogging, ½ hour
Saturday	First important race
Sunday	Jogging 1 hour or more

Continuation of racing:

Monday	Easy fartlek running, ¾ hour
Tuesday	Relaxed striding, 4 x 200 meters
Wednesday	Race or time trials
Thursday	Repeat Monday's session
Friday	Repeat Tuesday's session
Saturday	Repeat Wednesday's session
Sunday	Jogging, 1 hour or more

3,000 METERS (BOYS, AGES 15–16)

For as long as possible:

Monday	Long aerobic running, 1 hour
Tuesday	Long aerobic running, 1 to 1½ hours
Wednesday	Time trials, 5,000 meters
Thursday	Repeat Tuesday's session
Friday	Easy fartlek running, ½ to ¾ hour
Saturday	Time trials, 10,000 meters
Sunday	Long aerobic running, 1¼ to 1½ hours

For 4 weeks:

Monday	Hill springing, steep hills or step running, ¾ hour
Tuesday	Long aerobic running, 1 to 1½ hours
Wednesday	Easy fartlek running, ¾ hour
Thursday	Repeat Monday's session
Friday	Leg speed, 8–10 x 100 meters
Saturday	Time trials, 5,000 meters
Sunday	Long aerobic running, 1¼ to 2 hours

For 4 weeks:

Monday	Time trials, 3,000 meters
Tuesday	Repetitions, 8–12 x 400 meters
Wednesday	Long aerobic running, 1 to 1½ hours
Thursday	Repetitions, 8–12 x 200 meters
Friday	Leg speed, 8–10 x 100 meters
Saturday	Time trials, 5,000 meters
Sunday	Long aerobic running, 1 to 1½ hours

For 4 weeks:

Monday	6–10 x 100-meter wind sprints (one every 200 meters)
Tuesday	Easy fartlek running, ¾ hour
Wednesday	Time trials, 200 meters; pace-judgement running, hill springing
Thursday	Jogging, 1 hour
Friday	Relaxed striding, 3 x 300 meters
Saturday	Race, 1,500 or 3,000 meters
Sunday	Long aerobic running, 1 to 1½ hours

For 1 week:

Monday	12–16 x 45-meter wind sprints (one every 100 meters)
Tuesday	Jogging, ¾ hour
Wednesday	Time trials, 3,000 meters, fast
Thursday	Easy fartlek running, ¾ hour
Friday	Relaxed striding, 3 x 200 meters
Saturday	Race, 3,000 meters
Sunday	Jogging, 1 hour

For 1 week:

Monday	12 x 45-meter wind sprints (one every 100 meters)
Tuesday	Easy fartlek running, ¾ hour
Wednesday	Time trials, 800 meters
Thursday	Jogging, ¾ hour
Friday	Jogging, ½ hour
Saturday	First important race
Sunday	Jogging, 1 to 1½ hours

Continuation of racing:

Monday	Easy fartlek running, ¾ hour
Tuesday	Relaxed striding, 4 x 200 meters
Wednesday	Race, 200 meters; pace judgement running, hill springing
Thursday	Repeat Monday's session
Friday	Jogging, ½ hour
Saturday	Race or time trials
Sunday	Jogging, 1 to 1½ hours

3,000 METERS (GIRLS, AGES 15–17)

For as long as possible:

Monday	Easy fartlek running, ½ to ¾ hour
Tuesday	Long aerobic running, 1 to 1¼ hours
Wednesday	Time trials, 5,000 meters
Thursday	Repeat Tuesday's session
Friday	Easy fartlek running, ½ hour
Saturday	Time trials, 5,000 meters
Sunday	Long aerobic running, 1¼ hours or more

For 4 weeks:

Monday	Hill springing, steep hills or step running, ½ to ¾ hour
Tuesday	Long aerobic running, 1 to 1¼ hours
Wednesday	Easy fartlek running, ½ to ¾ hour
Thursday	Repeat Monday's session
Friday	Leg speed, 6–8 x 100 meters
Saturday	Time trials, 5,000 meters
Sunday	Long aerobic running, 1½ hours or more

For 4 weeks:

Monday	Time trials, 3,000 meters
Tuesday	Repetitions, 8–12 x 400 meters
Wednesday	Long aerobic running, 1 to 1¼ hours
Thursday	Repetitions, 8–12 x 200 meters
Friday	Leg speed, 6–8 x 100 meters
Saturday	Time trials, 5,000 meters
Sunday	Long aerobic running, 1½ hours or more

For 4 weeks:

Monday	6–8 x 45-meter wind sprints (one every 100 meters)
Tuesday	Easy fartlek running, ½ to ¾ hour
Wednesday	Time trials, 200 meters and middle distance
Thursday	Jogging, 1 hour
Friday	Relaxed striding, 3 x 300 meters
Saturday	Race, 1,500 or 3,000 meters
Sunday	Long aerobic running, 1 hour or more

For 1 week:

Monday	12–16 x 45-meter wind sprints (one every 100 meters)
Tuesday	Jogging, ¾ hour
Wednesday	Time trials, 3,000 meters, fast
Thursday	Easy fartlek running, ½ hour
Friday	Relaxed striding, 3 x 200 meters
Saturday	Race, 1,500 meters
Sunday	Jogging, 1 hour

For 1 week:

Monday	12 x 45-meter wind sprints (one every 100 meters)
Tuesday	Easy fartlek running, ½ hour
Wednesday	Time trials, 800 meters
Thursday	Jogging, ½ hour
Friday	Jogging, ½ hour
Saturday	First important race
Sunday	Jogging, 1 hour or more

Continuation of racing:

Monday	Easy fartlek running, ½ to ¾ hour
Tuesday	Relaxed striding, 4 x 200 meters
Wednesday	Race, 200 meters, or middle distances
Thursday	Repeat Monday's session
Friday	Jogging, ½ hour
Saturday	Race or time trial
Sunday	Jogging, 1 hour or more

3,000 METERS (WOMEN)

For as long as possible:

Monday	Easy fartlek running, ¾ to 1 hour
Tuesday	Long aerobic running, 1 to 1½ hours
Wednesday	Time trials, 5,000 meters
Thursday	Repeat Tuesday's session
Friday	Easy fartlek running, ¾ hour
Saturday	Time trials, 10,000 meters
Sunday	Long aerobic running, 1½ hours or more

For 4 weeks:

Monday	Hill springing, steep hills or step running, ¾ to 1 hour
Tuesday	Long aerobic running, 1 to 1½ hours
Wednesday	Easy fartlek running, ¾ to 1 hour
Thursday	Repeat Monday's session
Friday	Leg speed, 10 x 100 meters
Saturday	Time trials, 5,000 meters
Sunday	Long aerobic running, 1½ to 2 hours

For 4 weeks:

Monday	Time trials, 3,000 meters
Tuesday	Repetitions, 10–15 x 400 meters
Wednesday	Long aerobic running, 1 to 1½ hours
Thursday	Repetitions, 12–18 x 200 meters
Friday	Leg speed, 10 x 100 meters
Saturday	Time trials, 5,000 meters
Sunday	Long aerobic running, 1½ hours or more

For 4 weeks:

Monday	8–10 x 100-meter wind sprints (one every 200 meters)
Tuesday	Easy fartlek running, ¾ to 1 hour
Wednesday	Time trials, 200 meters and middle distance
Thursday	Jogging, 1 hour
Friday	Relaxed running, 3 x 300 meters
Saturday	Race, 1,500 or 3,000 meters
Sunday	Long aerobic running, 1½ hours or more

For 1 week:

Monday	12–16 x 45-meter wind sprints (one every 100 meters)
Tuesday	Jogging, 1 hour
Wednesday	Time trials, 3,000 meters
Thursday	Easy fartlek running, ½ to ¾ hours
Friday	Relaxed striding, 3 x 200 meters
Saturday	Race, 1,500 meters
Sunday	Jogging, 1 hour

For 1 week:

Monday	12 x 45-meter wind sprints (one every 100 meters)
Tuesday	Easy fartlek running, ¾ hour
Wednesday	Time trials, 800 meters
Thursday	Jogging, ¾ hour
Friday	Jogging, ½ hour
Saturday	First important race
Sunday	Jogging, 1 to 1½ hours

Continuation of racing:

Monday	Easy fartlek running, ¾ hour
Tuesday	Relaxed striding, 4 x 200 meters
Wednesday	Race, 200 meters or middle distance
Thursday	Repeat Monday's session
Friday	Jogging, ½ hour
Saturday	Race or time trials
Sunday	Jogging, 1 to 1½ hours

5,000 AND 10,000 METERS (AGES 17–18)

For as long as possible:

Monday	Easy fartlek running, ¾ to 1 hour
Tuesday	Long aerobic running, 1 to 1½ hours
Wednesday	Time trials, 5,000 meters
Thursday	Repeat Tuesday's session
Friday	Repeat Monday's session
Saturday	Time trials, 10,000 meters
Sunday	Long aerobic running, 1½ hours or more

For 4 weeks:

Monday	Leg speed, 8–10 x 100 meters
Tuesday	Long aerobic running, 1 to 1½ hours
Wednesday	Hill springing, steep hills or step running, ¾ hour
Thursday	Repeat Tuesday's session
Friday	Repeat Monday's session
Saturday	Repeat Wednesday's session
Sunday	Long aerobic running, 1½ hours or more

For 4 weeks:

Monday	Repetitions, 10–15 x 400 meters
Tuesday	Long aerobic running, 1 to 1½ hours
Wednesday	Easy fartlek running, ¾ hour
Thursday	Repetitions, 12–16 x 400 meters
Friday	Leg speed, 6–8 x 100 meters
Saturday	Time trials, 5,000 meters
Sunday	Long aerobic running, 1½ hours or more

For 4 weeks:

Monday	8–10 x 100-meter wind sprints (one every 200 meters)
Tuesday	Long aerobic running, 1 to 1½ hours
Wednesday	Time trials, 200 and 800 meters, or 1,500 meters
Thursday	Easy fartlek running, ¾ hour
Friday	Fast relaxed running, 4 x 100 meters
Saturday	Race, 3,000 meters or 1,500 meters
Sunday	Jogging, 1 hour or more

For 1 week:

Monday	16 x 45-meter wind sprints (one every 100 meters)
Tuesday	Easy fartlek running, ¾ hour
Wednesday	Time trials, race distance
Thursday	Easy fartlek running, ½ hour
Friday	Relaxed striding, 4 x 200 meters
Saturday	Race, 1,500 meters
Sunday	Long aerobic running, 1 hour

For 1 week:

Monday	12–16 x 45-meter wind sprints (one every 100 meters)
Tuesday	Easy fartlek running, ½ hour
Wednesday	Time trials, 800 meters
Thursday	Jogging, ½ hour
Friday	Repeat Thursday's session
Saturday	First important race
Sunday	Jogging, 1 to 1½ hours

Continuation of racing:

Monday	Easy fartlek running, 1 hour
Tuesday	Relaxed striding, 4 x 200 meters
Wednesday	Race or time trials
Thursday	Repeat Monday's session
Friday	Repeat Tuesday's session
Saturday	Race or time trials
Sunday	Jogging, 1 to 1½ hours

5,000 AND 10,000 METERS (AGES 18–20)

For as long as possible:

Monday	Easy fartlek running, ¾ to 1 hour
Tuesday	Long aerobic running, 1½ hours
Wednesday	Time trials, 5,000 meters
Thursday	Repeat Tuesday's session
Friday	Easy fartlek running, ¾ hour
Saturday	Time trials, 10,000 meters
Sunday	Long aerobic running, 2 hours

For 4 weeks:

Monday	Leg speed, 10 x 100 meters
Tuesday	Long aerobic running, 1½ hours
Wednesday	Hill springing, steep hills or step running, ¾ to 1 hour
Thursday	Repeat Tuesday's session
Friday	Repeat Monday's session
Saturday	Repeat Thursday's session
Sunday	Long aerobic running, 2 hours

For 4 weeks:

Monday	Repetitions, 12—16 x 400 meters
Tuesday	Long aerobic running, 1½ hours
Wednesday	Easy fartlek running, ¾ to 1 hour
Thursday	Repetitions, 15—20 x 200 meters
Friday	Leg speed, 8 x 100 meters
Saturday	Time trials, 5,000 meters
Sunday	Long aerobic running, 2 hours

For 4 weeks:

Monday	10–12 x 100-meter wind sprints (one every 200 meters)
Tuesday	Long aerobic running, 1½ hours
Wednesday	Time trials, 200 and 800 meters; or 1,500 meters
Thursday	Easy fartlek running, ¾ hour
Friday	Fast relaxed running, 4 x 100 meters
Saturday	Race, 3,000 meters or 5,000 meters
Sunday	Jogging, 1½ hours

For 1 week:

Monday	16–20 x 45-meter wind sprints (one every 100 meters)
Tuesday	Easy fartlek running, ¾ hour
Wednesday	Time trials, race distance
Thursday	Repeat Tuesday's session
Friday	Relaxed striding, 4 x 200 meters
Saturday	Race, 1,500 meters
Sunday	Jogging, 1½ hours

For 1 week:

Monday	12–16 x 45-meter wind sprints (one every 100 meters)
Tuesday	Easy fartlek running, ¾ hour
Wednesday	Time trials, 800 meters
Thursday	Jogging, ¾ hour
Friday	Jogging, ½ hour
Saturday	First important race
Sunday	Jogging, 1½ hours

Continuation of running:

Monday	Easy fartlek running, 1 hour
Tuesday	Relaxed striding, 4 x 200 meters
Wednesday	Race or time trial
Thursday	Easy fartlek running, ¾ hour
Friday	Repeat Tuesday's session
Saturday	Race or time trial
Sunday	Jogging, 1½ hours or more

5,000 AND 10,000 METERS (ADULTS)

For as long as possible:

Monday	Easy fartlek running, 1 hour
Tuesday	Long aerobic running, 1½ hours
Wednesday	Time trials, 10,000 meters
Thursday	Repeat Tuesday's session
Friday	Repeat Monday's session
Saturday	Repeat Wednesday's session
Sunday	Long aerobic running, 2 hours or more

For 4 weeks:

Monday	Leg speed, 10 x 120 meters
Tuesday	Long aerobic running, 1½ hours
Wednesday	Hill springing, steep hills or step running, 1 hour
Thursday	Repeat Tuesday's session
Friday	Repeat Monday's session
Saturday	Repeat Wednesday's session
Sunday	Long aerobic running, 2 hours or more

For 4 weeks:

Monday	Repetitions, 15–20 x 400 meters
Tuesday	Long aerobic running, 1½ hours
Wednesday	Easy fartlek running, 1 hour
Thursday	Repetitions, 15–20 x 200 meters
Friday	Leg speed, 10 x 100 meters
Saturday	Time trials, 5,000 or 10,000 meters
Sunday	Long aerobic running, 2 hours or more

For 4 weeks:

Monday	12–14 x 100-meter wind sprints (one every 200 meters)
Tuesday	Long aerobic running, 1½ hours
Wednesday	Time trials, 200 and 800 meters, or 1,500 meters
Thursday	Easy fartlek running, 1 hour
Friday	Fast relaxed running, 6 x 100 meters
Saturday	Race, 3,000, 5,000, or 10,000 meters
Sunday	Jogging, 1½ or 2 hours

For 1 week:

Monday	20 x 45-meter wind sprints (one every 100 meters)
Tuesday	Easy fartlek running, 1 hour
Wednesday	Time trials, race distance
Thursday	Easy fartlek running, ¾ hour
Friday	Relaxed striding, 6 x 200 meters
Saturday	Race, 1,500 meters
Sunday	Jogging, 1½ hours

For 1 week:

Monday	16 x 45-meter wind sprints (one every 100 meters)
Tuesday	Easy fartlek running, ¾ hour
Wednesday	Time trials, 800 meters
Thursday	Jogging, ¾ hour
Friday	Jogging, ½ hour
Saturday	First important race
Sunday	Jogging, 1½ hours

Continuation of racing:

Monday	Easy fartlek running, 1 hour
Tuesday	Relaxed striding, 6 x 200 meters
Wednesday	Race or time trials, 3,000 meters
Thursday	Repeat Monday's session
Friday	Repeat Tuesday's session
Saturday	Race or time trials, 5,000 meters
Sunday	Jogging, 1½ hours

3,000-METER STEEPLECHASE (MEN)

For as long as possible:

Monday	Easy fartlek running, 1 hour
Tuesday	Long aerobic running, 1½ hours
Wednesday	Time trials, 5,000 meters
Thursday	Repeat Tuesday's session
Friday	Easy fartlek running, ¾ hours (hills)
Saturday	Time trials, 10,000 meters
Sunday	Long aerobic running, 1½ hours or more

For 4 weeks:

Monday	Leg speed, 10 x 100 meters
Tuesday	Long aerobic running, 1½ hours
Wednesday	Hill springing, steep hills or step running, 1 hour
Thursday	Easy fartlek, 1 hour
Friday	Repeat Monday's session
Saturday	Repeat Wednesday's session
Sunday	Long aerobic running, 1½ hours or more

For 4 weeks:

Monday	Repetitions, 15–20 x 400 meters
Tuesday	Time trials, 3,000 meters; hurdles practice at ¾ effort
Wednesday	Easy fartlek running, 1 hour
Thursday	Repetitions, 15–20 x 200 meters
Friday	High knee-lift exercises, long striding exercises, running-tall exercises, 2 x 100 meters; fast relaxed running, 6 x 100 meters
Saturday	Time trials, 5,000 or 3,000 meters; hurdles practice, water jump practice
Sunday	Long aerobic running, 1½ hours or more

For 4 weeks:

Monday	10–12 x 100-meter wind sprints (one every 200 meters) meters)
Tuesday	Time trials, 300 meters and hurdles practice at ¾ effort
Wednesday	Time trials, 200 meters and 800 meters
Thursday	Easy fartlek running, 1 hour
Friday	Hurdles practice, water jump practice, ½ hour

Saturday	Race; 1,500, 3,000, or 5,000 meters
Sunday	Jogging, 1½ hours

For 1 week:

Monday	20 x 45-meter wind sprints (one every 100 meters)
Tuesday	Easy fartlek running, 1 hour
Wednesday	Time trials, 3,000 meters; hurdles practice, fast
Thursday	Long aerobic running, ¾ hour
Friday	Relaxed striding, 4 x 200 meters; hurdles practice and water jump practice
Saturday	Race, 800 or 1,500 meters
Sunday	Jogging, 1 to 1½ hours

For 1 week:

Monday	12–16 x 45-meter wind sprints (one every 100 meters)
Tuesday	Easy fartlek running; ¾ hour
Wednesday	Time trials, 100 and 400 meters
Thursday	Hurdles practice and jogging, ½ hour
Friday	Jogging, ½ hour
Saturday	First important race
Sunday	Jogging, 1½ hours

Continuation of racing:

Monday	Easy fartlek running, ¾ to 1 hour
Tuesday	Relaxed striding, 4 x 200 meters; hurdles practice
Wednesday	Race or time trial
Thursday	Easy fartlek running, ¾ hour
Friday	Repeat Tuesday's session
Saturday	Race or time trials
Sunday	Jogging, 1 to 1½ hours

Cross-Country

There is often a need for cross-country runners to race early in the season to support their school or club teams. So it may become necessary to develop some anaerobic exercise ability while trying to improve your general condition. For this, it is best to use easy fartlek sessions and time trials, which can be incorporated into the early conditioning schedule. This is not the best way to train, but it may be essential for cross-country runners.

The fartlek should be of a relatively easy effort, with concentration on individual weaknesses. Sessions can include steep hill running with a high knee action, for strengthening the legs, quadriceps, and ankles; hill springing for ankle flexibility and power; and striding out downhill or across flat areas. Don't overdo the anaerobic sprints so that the session becomes a hard anaerobic workout.

The time trials should be run strongly and evenly, on terrain similar to what you will eventually race over, or on a grass track if even-paced running is desired. Don't run at your best effort, but rather about seven-eighths effort, always knowing you could do a little better and are holding something in reserve.

Since this is only a guide, use common sense in applying the schedule. If your legs feel dead after racing, jog a few days until they have recovered, avoiding speed work. Recovery is important in cross-country because the terrain you race over can pull your legs about.

Control anaerobic training carefully. Practice clearing fences similar to those you experience in racing. This gives full confidence. Run over soft and sandy ground as often as possible to accustom yourself to relaxing and not driving too hard with the legs. Try to develop a pulling action, with the hips comfortably forward. Cut down your stride length a little. Leg speed should increase.

Jog most mornings as a supplement to your main training sessions. Try to incorporate in them a little steep hill running, hill springing, and step running. Even 15 minutes will help to condition your legs and increase your speed later.

BOYS UNDER AGE 12

For as long as possible:

Monday	Long aerobic running, ¼ to ½ hour
Tuesday	Easy fartlek running, ¼ to ½ hour
Wednesday	Time trials, 2,000 meters
Thursday	Repeat Monday's session
Friday	Jogging, ¼ hour; or rest
Saturday	Time trials, 2,000 meters
Sunday	Long aerobic running, ½ hour or more

For 4 weeks:

Monday	Easy fartlek running, ¼ to ½ hour
Tuesday	Long aerobic running, ¼ to ½ hour
Wednesday	Time trials, 2,000 meters
Thursday	Relaxed striding, 4 x 150 meters
Friday	Jogging, ¼ hour; or rest
Saturday	Time trials, 2,000 meters
Sunday	Long aerobic running, ½ hour or more

For 4 weeks:

Monday	6–8 x 45-meter wind sprints (one every 100 meters)
Tuesday	Easy fartlek running, ¼ to ½ hour
Wednesday	Time trials, 1,500 meters
Thursday	Easy fartlek running, ¼ to ½ hour
Friday	Jogging, ¼ hour; or rest
Saturday	Development races
Sunday	Jogging, ½ hour or more

For 1 week:

Monday	6–8 x 45-meter wind sprints (one every 100 meters)
Tuesday	Easy fartlek running, ½ hour
Wednesday	Time trials, 800 meters
Thursday	Relaxed striding, 4 x 150 meters
Friday	Rest
Saturday	Race, 2,000 meters
Sunday	Jogging, ½ to ¾ hour

For 1 week:

Monday	6–8 x 45-meter wind sprints (one every 100 meters)
Tuesday	Easy fartlek running, ¼ to ½ hour
Wednesday	Time trials, 800 meters
Thursday	Jogging, ½ hour
Friday	Jogging, ¼ hour; or rest
Saturday	Race, 1,000 meters
Sunday	Jogging, ½ to ¾ hour

For 1 week:

Monday	6–8 x 45-meter wind sprints (one every 100 meters)
Tuesday	Jogging, ½ hour
Wednesday	Time trials, 600 meters
Thursday	Jogging, ¼ hour
Friday	Rest
Saturday	First important race
Sunday	Jogging, ½ hour or more

Continuation of racing:

Monday	6–8 x 45 meter wind sprints (one every 100 meters)
Tuesday	Easy fartlek running, ¼ to ½ hour
Wednesday	Time trials, 800 meters
Thursday	Repeat Tuesday's session
Friday	Jogging, ¼ hour; or rest
Saturday	Race
Sunday	Jogging, ½ hour or more

GIRLS UNDER AGE 12

For as long as possible:

Monday	Long aerobic running, ¼ to ½ hour
Tuesday	Easy fartlek running, ¼ to ½ hour
Wednesday	Time trials, 2,000 meters
Thursday	Repeat Monday's session
Friday	Jogging, ¼ hour; or rest
Saturday	Repeat Wednesday's session
Sunday	Long aerobic running, 20 minutes or more

For 4 weeks:

Monday	Easy fartlek running, ¼ to ½ hour or more
Tuesday	Long aerobic running, ¼ to ½ hour
Wednesday	Time trials, 2,000 meters
Thursday	Relaxed striding, 4 x 150 meters
Friday	Jogging, ¼ hour or rest
Saturday	Time trials, 2,000 meters
Sunday	Long aerobic running, 20 minutes or more

For 4 weeks:

Monday	6–8 x 45-meter wind sprints (one every 100 meters)
Tuesday	Easy fartlek running, ¼ to ½ hour
Wednesday	Time trials, 2,000 meters
Thursday	Repeat Tuesday's session
Friday	Jogging, ¼ hour or rest
Saturday	Development races
Sunday	Jogging, ½ hour

For 1 week:

Monday	6–8 x 45-meter wind sprints (one every 100 meters)
Tuesday	Easy fartlek running, ¼ to ½ hour
Wednesday	Time trials, 800 meters
Thursday	Relaxed striding, 3 x 800 meters
Friday	Jogging, ¼ hour or rest
Saturday	Race 2,000 meters
Sunday	Jogging, ½ hour

For 1 week:

Monday	6–8 x 45-meter wind sprints (one every 100 meters)
Tuesday	Easy fartlek running, ¼ to ½ hour
Wednesday	Time trials, 600 meters
Thursday	Jogging, ¼ hour
Friday	Jogging, ¼ hour or rest
Saturday	Race, 1,000 meters
Sunday	Jogging, ½ hour

For 1 week:

Monday	6 x 45-meter wind sprints (one every 100 meters)
Tuesday	Jogging, ¼ hour
Wednesday	Time trials, 600 meters
Thursday	Repeat Tuesday's session
Friday	Rest
Saturday	First important race
Sunday	Jogging, ½ hour

Continuation of racing:

Monday	6 x 45-meter wind sprints (one every 100 meters)
Tuesday	Easy fartlek running, ¼ to ½ hour
Wednesday	Time trials, 800 meters
Thursday	Repeat Tuesday's session
Friday	Jogging, ¼ hour or rest
Saturday	Race
Sunday	Jogging, ½ hour

BOYS AGE 12–13

For as long as possible:

Monday	Long aerobic running, ½ to ¾ hour
Tuesday	Easy fartlek running, ½ hour
Wednesday	Time trials, 3,000 meters
Thursday	Repeat Monday's session
Friday	Leg speed, 4–6 x 80 meters
Saturday	Repeat Wednesday's session
Sunday	Long aerobic running, ¾ to 1¼ hours

For 4 weeks:

Monday	Hill springing, steep hills or step running, ½ hour
Tuesday	Long aerobic running, ½ to 1 hour
Wednesday	Time trials, 3,000 meters
Thursday	Repetitions, 4–6 x 200 meters
Friday	Leg speed, 4–6 x 80 meters
Saturday	Repeat Wednesday's session
Sunday	Long aerobic running, ¾ to 1¼ hours

For 1 week:

Monday	8–10 x 45-meter wind sprints (one every 100 meters)
Tuesday	Easy fartlek running, ½ hour
Wednesday	Time trials, 1,000 meters
Thursday	Relaxed striding, 3 x 200 meters
Friday	Jogging, ½ hour
Saturday	Race, 2,500 meters
Sunday	Jogging, ¾ hour

For 1 week:

Monday	8 x 45-meter wind sprints (one every 100 meters)
Tuesday	Easy fartlek running, ½ hour
Wednesday	Time trials, 800 meters
Thursday	Repeat Tuesday's session
Friday	Jogging, ½ hour
Saturday	Race, 1,500 meters
Sunday	Jogging, ½ to ¾ hour

For 1 week:

Monday	8 x 45-meter wind sprints (one every 100 meters)
Tuesday	Long aerobic running, ½ hour
Wednesday	Time trials, 600 meters
Thursday	Jogging, ½ hour
Friday	Jogging, ½ hour; or rest
Saturday	First important race
Sunday	Jogging, ¾ hour or more

Continuation of racing:

Monday	8 x 45-meter wind sprints (one every 100 meters)
Tuesday	Easy fartlek running, ½ hour
Wednesday	Time trials, 800 meters
Thursday	Repeat Tuesday's session
Friday	Jogging, ½ hour
Saturday	Race
Sunday	Jogging, ¾ hour or more

GIRLS AGE 12–13

For as long as possible:

Monday	Long aerobic running, ½ to ¾ hour
Tuesday	Easy fartlek running, ¼ to ½ hour
Wednesday	Time trials, 2,500 meters
Thursday	Repeat Monday's session
Friday	Leg speed, 4–6 x 80 meters
Saturday	Time trials, 3,000 meters
Sunday	Long aerobic running, ½ hour or more

For 4 weeks:

Monday	Hill springing, steep hills or step running, ¼ hour
Tuesday	Long aerobic running, ½ to ¾ hour
Wednesday	Time trials, 2,500 meters
Thursday	Repetitions, 4–6 x 200 meters
Friday	Leg speed, 4–6 x 80 meters
Saturday	Time trials, 3,000 meters
Sunday	Long aerobic running, ½ hour or more

For 4 weeks:

Monday	4–6 x 100-meter wind sprints (one every 200 meters)
Tuesday	Easy fartlek running, ¼ to ½ hour
Wednesday	Time trials, 2,000 meters
Thursday	Repeat Tuesday's session
Friday	Jogging, ¼ hour or rest
Saturday	Development races
Sunday	Long aerobic running, ½ hour or more

For 1 week:

Monday	8–10 x 45-meter wind sprints (one every 100 meters)
Tuesday	Easy fartlek running, ¼ to ½ hour
Wednesday	Time trials, 800 meters
Thursday	Relaxed striding, 3 x 150 meters
Friday	Jogging, ¼ hour; or rest
Saturday	Race, 2,000 meters
Sunday	Jogging, ½ hour or more

For 1 week:

Monday	6–8 x 45-meter wind sprints (one every 100 meters)
Tuesday	Easy fartlek running, ¼ to ½ hour
Wednesday	Time trials, 600 meters
Thursday	Repeat Tuesday's session
Friday	Jogging, ¼ hour; or rest
Saturday	Race, 1,000 meters
Sunday	Jogging, ½ hour

For 1 week:

Monday	6 x 45-meter wind sprints (one every 100 meters)
Tuesday	Jogging, ½ hour
Wednesday	Time trials, 600 meters
Thursday	Jogging, ¼ hour
Friday	Rest
Saturday	First important race
Sunday	Jogging, ½ hour or more

Continuation of racing:

Monday	6–8 x 45-meter wind sprints (one every 100 meters)
Tuesday	Easy fartlek running, ¼ to ½ hour
Wednesday	Time trials, 600 meters
Thursday	Repeat Tuesday's session
Friday	Jogging, ¼ hour; or rest
Saturday	Race
Sunday	Jogging, ½ hour or more

BOYS AGE 14–15

For as long as possible:

Monday	Easy fartlek running, ½ to ¾ hour
Tuesday	Long aerobic running, ¾ to 1 hour
Wednesday	Time trials, 5,000 meters
Thursday	Repeat Tuesday's session
Friday	Leg speed, 6 x 100 meters
Saturday	Time trials, 3,000 meters
Sunday	Long aerobic running, 1 hour or more

For 4 weeks:

Monday	Hill springing, steep hills or step running, ½ to ¾ hour
Tuesday	Long aerobic running, ¾ to 1 hour
Wednesday	Time trials, 3,000 meters
Thursday	Repetitions, 6–8 x 200 meters
Friday	Leg speed, 6 x 100 meters
Saturday	Time trials, 3,000 meters
Sunday	Long aerobic running, 1 hour or more

For 4 weeks:

Monday	6–8 x 100-meter wind sprints (one every 200 meters)
Tuesday	Easy fartlek running, ½ to ¾ hour
Wednesday	Time trials, 3,000 meters
Thursday	Easy fartlek running, ½ hour
Friday	Relaxed striding, 4 x 200 meters
Saturday	Development races
Sunday	Long aerobic running, ¾ hour or more

For 1 week:

Monday	10–12 x 45-meter wind sprints (one every 100 meters)
Tuesday	Easy fartlek running, ½ hour
Wednesday	Time trials, 1,000 meters
Thursday	Repeat Tuesday's session
Friday	Jogging, ½ hour
Saturday	Race 3,000 meters
Sunday	Jogging, ¼ hour

For 1 week:

Monday	8–10 x 45-meter wind sprints (one every 100 meters)
Tuesday	Easy fartlek running, ½ hour
Wednesday	Time trials, 1,000 meters
Thursday	Repeat Tuesday's session
Friday	Relaxed striding, 3 x 200 meters
Saturday	Race, 2,000 meters
Sunday	Jogging, ¾ hours

For 1 week:

Monday	8 x 45-meter wind sprints (one every 100 meters)
Tuesday	Easy fartlek running, ½ hour
Wednesday	Time trials, 800 meters
Thursday	Jogging, ½ hour
Friday	Jogging, ½ hour or rest
Saturday	First important race
Sunday	Jogging, ¾ hour or more

Continuation of racing:

Monday	8–10 x 45-meter wind sprints (one every 100 meters)
Tuesday	Easy fartlek running, ½ to ¾ hour
Wednesday	Time trials, 1,000 meters
Thursday	Easy fartlek running, ½ hour
Friday	Jogging, ½ hour
Saturday	Race
Sunday	Jogging, ¾ hour or more

GIRLS AGE 14–15

For as long as possible:

Monday	Easy fartlek running, ½ hour
Tuesday	Long aerobic running, ¾ to 1 hour
Wednesday	Time trials, 3,000 meters
Thursday	Repeat Tuesday's session
Friday	Leg speed, 4–6 x 80 meters
Saturday	Time trials, 3,000 meters
Sunday	Long aerobic running, ¾ hour or more

For 4 weeks:

Monday	Hill springing, steep hills or step running, ½ hour
Tuesday	Long aerobic running, ¾ to 1 hour
Wednesday	Time trials, 3,000 meters
Thursday	Repetitions, 6–8 x 200 meters
Friday	Leg speed, 6–8 x 80 meters
Saturday	Time trials, 3,000 meters or club run
Sunday	Long aerobic running, ¾ hour or more

For 4 weeks:

Monday	6–8 x 100-meter wind sprints (one every 200 meters)
Tuesday	Easy fartlek running, ½ to ¾ hour
Wednesday	Time trials, 2,000 meters
Thursday	Easy fartlek running, ½ hour
Friday	Relaxed striding, 4 x 200 meters
Saturday	Development races
Sunday	Long aerobic running, ¾ hour or more

For 1 week:

Monday	8–10 x 45-meter wind sprints (one every 100 meters)
Tuesday	Easy fartlek running, ½ hour
Wednesday	Time trials, 1,000 meters
Thursday	Repeat Tuesday's session
Friday	Jogging, ½ hour
Saturday	Race, 2,500 meters
Sunday	Jogging, ¾ to 1 hour

For 1 week:

Monday	6–8 x 45-meter wind sprints (one every 100 meters)
Tuesday	Easy fartlek running, ½ hour
Wednesday	Time trials, 800 meters
Thursday	Repeat Tuesday's session
Friday	Relaxed striding, 3 x 200 meters
Saturday	Race, 1,000 meters
Sunday	Jogging, ¾ hour

For 1 week:

Monday	6 x 45-meter wind sprints (one every 100 meters)
Tuesday	Easy fartlek running, ½ hour
Wednesday	Time trials, 600 meters
Thursday	Jogging, ½ hour
Friday	Jogging, ¼ hour; or rest
Saturday	First important race
Sunday	Jogging, 1 hour

Continuation of racing:

Monday	6–8 x 45-meter wind sprints (one every 100 meters)
Tuesday	Easy fartlek running, ½ to ¾ hour
Wednesday	Time trials, 800 or 1,000 meters
Thursday	Easy fartlek running, ½ hour
Friday	Jogging, ½ hour
Saturday	Race
Sunday	Jogging, 1 hour

BOYS AGE 16–17

For as long as possible:

Monday	Easy fartlek running, ¾ to 1 hour
Tuesday	Long aerobic running, 1 to 1½ hours
Wednesday	Time trials, 5,000 meters
Thursday	Repeat Tuesday's session
Friday	Leg speed, 8–10 x 100 meters
Saturday	Repeat Wednesday's session
Sunday	Long aerobic running, 1½ hours or more

For 4 weeks:

Monday	Hill springings, steep hills or step running, ¾ hour
Tuesday	Long aerobic running, 1 to 1½ hours
Wednesday	Time trials, 5,000 meters
Thursday	Repeat Monday's session
Friday	Leg speed, 8–10 x 100 meters
Saturday	Repeat Wednesday's session
Sunday	Long aerobic running, 1½ hour or more

For 4 weeks:

Monday	6–8 x 100-meter wind sprints (one every 200 meters)
Tuesday	Easy fartlek running, ¾ to 1 hour
Wednesday	Time trials, 3,000 meters
Thursday	Repetitions, 8–10 x 200 meters
Friday	Relaxed striding, 4 x 300 meters
Saturday	Development races
Sunday	Long aerobic running, 1½ hour or more

For 1 week:

Monday	16 x 45-meter wind sprints (one every 100 meters)
Tuesday	Easy fartlek running, ¾ to 1 hour
Wednesday	Time trials, 3,000 meters
Thursday	Repetitions, 3 x 300 meters, fast
Friday	Jogging, ½ hour
Saturday	Race, 5,000 meters
Sunday	Jogging, 1 to 1½ hours

For 1 week:

Monday	16 x 45-meter wind sprints (one every 100 meters)
Tuesday	Easy fartlek running, ¾ hour
Wednesday	Time trials, 2,000 meters
Thursday	Easy fartlek running, ½ hour
Friday	Fast relaxed running, 3 x 200 meters
Saturday	Race, 3,000 meters
Sunday	Jogging, 1 hour

For 1 week:

Monday	12 x 45-meter wind sprints (one every 100 meters)
Tuesday	Easy fartlek running, ½ to ¾ hour
Wednesday	Time trials, 1,500 meters
Thursday	Jogging, ¾ hour
Friday	Jogging, ½ hour
Saturday	First important race
Sunday	Jogging, 1 to 1½ hours

Continuation of racing:

Monday	12–16 x 45-meter wind sprints (one every 100 meters)
Tuesday	Easy fartlek running, ¾ hour
Wednesday	Time trials, 3,000 meters
Thursday	Easy fartlek running, ½ hour
Friday	Jogging, ½ hour
Saturday	Race
Sunday	Jogging, 1 to 1½ hours

GIRLS AGE 16–17

For as long as possible:

Monday	Easy fartlek running, ¾ hour
Tuesday	Long aerobic running, 1 hour or more
Wednesday	Time trials, 4,000 meters
Thursday	Repeat Tuesday's session
Friday	Leg speed, 6–8 x 80 meters
Saturday	Time trials, 5,000 meters
Sunday	Repeat Tuesday's session

For 4 weeks:

Monday	Hill springing, steep hills or step running, ½ to ¾ hour
Tuesday	Long aerobic running, 1 hour or more
Wednesday	Time trials, 3,000 meters
Thursday	Repetitions, 8–10 x 200 meters
Friday	Leg speed, 8–10 x 80 meters
Saturday	Time trials, 4,000 meters
Sunday	Repeat Tuesday's session

For 4 weeks:

Monday	6–8 x 100-meter wind sprints (one every 200 meters)
Tuesday	Easy fartlek running, ¾ hour
Wednesday	Time trials, 3,000 meters
Thursday	Easy fartlek running, ½ hour
Friday	Relaxed striding, 4–6 x 200 meters
Saturday	Development races
Sunday	Long aerobic running, 1 hour or more

For 1 week:

Monday	12–16 x 45-meter wind sprints (one every 100 meters)
Tuesday	Easy fartlek running, ¾ hour
Wednesday	Time trials, 1,500 meters
Thursday	Easy fartlek running, ½ hour
Friday	Jogging, ½ hour
Saturday	Race, 3,000 meters
Sunday	Jogging, 1 hour

For 1 week:

Monday	12 x 45-meter wind sprints (one every 100 meters)
Tuesday	Easy fartlek running, ½ hour
Wednesday	Time trials, 1,000 meters
Thursday	Easy fartlek running, ½ hour
Friday	Relaxed striding, 3 x 200 meters
Saturday	Race, 200 meters
Sunday	Jogging, 1 hour

For 1 week:

Monday	12 x 45-meter wind sprints (one every 100 meters)
Tuesday	Easy fartlek running, ½ hour
Wednesday	Time trials, 600 meters
Thursday	Jogging, ½ hour
Friday	Jogging, ½ hour; or rest
Saturday	Frist important race
Sunday	Jogging, 1 hour

Continuation of racing:

Monday	6–8 x 45-meter wind sprints (one every 100 meters)
Tuesday	Easy fartlek running, ½ to ¾ hour
Wednesday	Time trials, 1,000 meters
Thursday	Easy fartlek running, ½ hour
Friday	Jogging, ½ hour
Saturday	Race
Sunday	Jogging, 1 hour or more

BOYS 18–19

For as long as possible:

Monday	Easy fartlek running, 1 hour
Tuesday	Long aerobic running, 1 to 1½ hours
Wednesday	Time trials, 5,000 meters
Thursday	Repeat Tuesday's session
Friday	Leg speed, 10 x 100 meters
Saturday	Time trials, 10,000 meters
Sunday	Long aerobic running, 1½ hours or more

For 4 weeks:

Monday	Hill springing, steep hills or step running, ¾ to 1 hour
Tuesday	Long aerobic running, 1 to 1½ hours
Wednesday	Time trials, 5,000 meters
Thursday	Repeat Monday's session
Friday	Leg speed, 10 x 100 meters
Saturday	Repeat Wednesday's session
Sunday	Long aerobic running, 1½ hours or more

For 4 weeks:

Monday	8–12 x 100-meter wind sprints (one every 200 meters)
Tuesday	Easy fartlek running, 1 hour
Wednesday	Time trials, 5,000 meters
Thursday	Repetitions, 10–12 x 200 meters
Friday	Relaxed striding, 4 x 300 meters
Saturday	Development races
Sunday	Long aerobic running, 1½ hours or more

For 1 week:

Monday	16–20 x 45-meter wind sprints (one every 100 meters)
Tuesday	Easy fartlek running, 1 hour
Wednesday	Time trials, 3,000 meters
Thursday	Easy fartlek running, ¾ hour
Friday	Jogging, ½ hour
Saturday	Race, 5,000 meters
Sunday	Jogging, 1½ hours

For 1 week:

Monday	16 x 45-meter wind sprints (one every 100 meters)
Tuesday	Easy fartlek running, ¾ hour
Wednesday	Time trials, 2,000 meters
Thursday	Easy fartlek running, ½ hour
Friday	Fast relaxed running, 3 x 200 meters
Saturday	Race, 3,000 meters
Sunday	Jogging, 1 hour

For 1 week:

Monday	16 x 45-meter wind sprints (one every 100 meters)
Tuesday	Easy fartlek running, ¾ hour
Wednesday	Time trials, 1,500 meters
Thursday	Jogging, ¾ hour
Friday	Jogging, ½ hour
Saturday	First important race
Sunday	Jogging, 1½ hours

Continuation of racing:

Monday	16 x 45-meter wind sprints (one every 100 meters)
Tuesday	Easy fartlek running, ¾ hour
Wednesday	Time trials, 3,000 meters
Thursday	Easy fartlek running, ½ hour
Friday	Jogging, ½ hour
Saturday	Race
Sunday	Jogging, 1½ hours

MEN

For as long as possible:

Monday	Easy fartlek running, 1 hour
Tuesday	Long aerobic running, 1½ hours
Wednesday	Time trials, 5,000 meters
Thursday	Repeat Tuesday's session
Friday	Leg speed, 10 x 100 meters
Saturday	Time trials, 10,000 meters
Sunday	Long aerobic running, 2 hours or more

For 4 weeks:

Monday	Hill springing, steep hills or step running, 1 hour
Tuesday	Long aerobic running, 1½ hours
Wednesday	Time trials, 5,000 meters
Thursday	Repeat Monday's session
Friday	Sprint training, 10 x 100 meters
Saturday	Time trials, 10,000 meters
Sunday	Long aerobic running, 2 hours or more

For 4 weeks:

Monday	10–12 x 100-meter wind sprints (one every 200 meters)
Tuesday	Easy fartlek running, 1 hour
Wednesday	Time trials, 5,000 meters
Thursday	Repetitions, 10–15 x 200 meters
Friday	Relaxed striding, 4 x 300 meters
Saturday	Development races
Sunday	Long aerobic running, 2 hours

For 1 week:

Monday	20 x 45-meter wind sprints (one every 100 meters)
Tuesday	Easy fartlek running, 1 hour
Wednesday	Time trials, 3,000 meters
Thursday	Easy fartlek running, ¾ hour
Friday	Jogging, ½ hour
Saturday	Race, 10,000 meters
Sunday	Jogging, 1½ hours

For 1 week:

Monday	20 x 45-meter wind sprints (one every 100 meters)
Tuesday	Easy fartlek running, ¾ hour
Wednesday	Time trials, 2,000 meters
Thursday	Easy fartlek running, ½ hour
Friday	Fast relaxed running, 3 x 200 meters
Saturday	Race, 3,000 meters
Sunday	Jogging, 1 hour

For 1 week:

Monday	16 x 45-meter wind sprints (one every 100 meters)
Tuesday	Easy fartlek running, ¾ hour
Wednesday	Time trials, 1,500 meters
Thursday	Jogging, ¾ hour
Friday	Jogging, ½ hour
Saturday	First important race
Sunday	Jogging, 1½ hours

Continuation of racing:

Monday	16 x 45-meter wind sprints (one every 100 meters)
Tuesday	Easy fartlek running, ¾ hour
Wednesday	Time trials, 3,000 meters
Thursday	Easy fartlek running, ½ hour
Friday	Jogging, ½ hour
Saturday	Race
Sunday	Jogging, 1½ hours or more

WOMEN

For as long as possible:

Monday	Easy fartlek running, ¾ to 1 hour
Tuesday	Long aerobic running, 1 to 1½ hours
Wednesday	Time trials, 5,000 meters
Thursday	Repeat Tuesday's session
Friday	Leg speed, 8–10 x 100 meters
Saturday	Repeat Wednesday's session
Sunday	Long aerobic running, 1½ hours or more

For 4 weeks:

Monday	Hill springings, steep hills or step running, ¾ to 1 hour
Tuesday	Long aerobic running, 1 to 1½ hours
Wednesday	Time trials, 3,000 meters
Thursday	Repeat Monday's session
Friday	Leg speed, 8–10 x 100 meters
Saturday	Time trials, 5,000 meters
Sunday	Long aerobic running, 1½ hours or more

For 4 weeks:

Monday	10–12 x 100-meter wind sprints (one every 200 meters)
Tuesday	Easy fartlek running, ¾ to 1 hour
Wednesday	Time trials, 3,000 meters
Thursday	Repetitions, 3 x 300 meters, fast
Friday	Relaxed striding, 4 x 300 meters
Saturday	Development races
Sunday	Long aerobic running, 1½ hours or more

For 1 week:

Monday	16–20 x 45-meter wind sprints (one every 100 meters)
Tuesday	Easy fartlek running, ¾ to 1 hour
Wednesday	Time trials, 2,000 meters
Thursday	Easy fartlek running, ¾ hour
Friday	Jogging, ½ hour
Saturday	Race, 5,000 meters
Sunday	Jogging, 1 hour

For 1 week:

Monday	16 x 45-meter wind sprints (one every 100 meters)
Tuesday	Easy fartlek running, ¾ hour
Wednesday	Time trials, 2,000 meters
Thursday	Easy fartlek running, ½ hour
Friday	Fast relaxed running, 3 x 200 meters
Saturday	Race, 2,000 meters
Sunday	Jogging, 1 hour

For 1 week:

Monday	16 x 45-meter wind sprints (one every 100 meters)
Tuesday	Easy fartlek running, ½ hour
Wednesday	Time trials, 1,000 meters
Thursday	Jogging, ¾ hour
Friday	Jogging, ½ hour
Saturday	First important race
Sunday	Jogging, 1½ hours

Continuation of racing:

Monday	16 x 45-meter wind sprints (one every 100 meters)
Tuesday	Easy fartlek running, ¾ hour
Wednesday	Time trials, 3,000 meters
Thursday	Easy fartlek running, ½ hour
Friday	Jogging, ½ hour
Saturday	Race
Sunday	Jogging, 1 hour or more

Marathon

The goal of marathon training is to develop fine general cardiac efficiency, which basically means improving intake, transportation, and utilization of oxygen. With continued running, the intake and transportation improve quickly, but improvement in utilization by the muscles takes longer. This necessary aspect of muscular endurance can only be brought about through continuous exercise of muscle groups for long periods. Muscle-group exercise, particularly for periods of 2 hours or more, not only affects underdeveloped capillary beds but also develops new beds, increasing muscular endurance. So, to be successful in marathon racing or running, it is essential to go for long runs often—the more the better.

The nucleus of the marathon training schedule is three long runs a week, interchanged with other runs that, while they can be shorter, are usually over hilly terrain. Because marathons are run most of the way at fast aerobic efforts, there is normally little need to do a lot of anaerobic training. This means that to develop the anaerobic capacity to race marathons, time trials at 5,000 and 10,000 meters are sufficient.

The use of fartlek or speed-play training is of value. Fartlek training is done by mixing all sorts of running over golf course-type terrain. Set yourself a length of time to train and, once you are warmed up, stride out fast, sprint, sprint up hills, stride down hills, jog, and generally run according to how you feel.

When you begin marathon training, it is better to train on a time basis rather than set out to cover a given mileage. This allows you to feel your way and avoid biting off too much at the beginning. Always run to your individual fitness level. That can involve anaerobic running. In conditioning training, you can never run too slow to improve the oxygen uptake; but you can run too fast. Train well within your capabilities. Start your races at steady effort, and don't be trapped into going too fast at the beginning.

Getting used to running in heat is important; if you're not prepared for it you can suffer ill-effects. Hot-weather training develops the skin arterioles, which allow more blood to be pumped to the skin surface for cooling. Sauna baths can help in this development.

A modified marathon schedule for women is included in chapter 14.

BEGINNERS

For as long as possible:

Monday	Long aerobic running, ½ to ¾ hour
Tuesday	Long aerobic running, 1 hour
Wednesday	Repeat Monday's session
Thursday	Repeat Tuesday's session
Friday	Repeat Monday's session
Saturday	Long aerobic running, 1 to 2 hours
Sunday	Long aerobic running, ¾ to 1 hour

For 6 weeks:

Monday	Long aerobic running, ¾ to 1 hour
Tuesday	Long aerobic running, 1 to 1½ hours
Wednesday	Easy fartlek running, ½ to ¾ hour
Thursday	Repeat Tuesday's session
Friday	Easy fartlek running, ½ hour
Saturday	Long aerobic running, 1½ to 2 hours
Sunday	Repeat Monday's session

For 6 weeks:

Monday	Time trials, 5,000 meters
Tuesday	Long aerobic running, 1 to 1½ hours
Wednesday	Time trials, 10,000 meters
Thursday	Repeat Tuesday's session
Friday	Easy fartlek running, ½ to ¾ hour
Saturday	Long aerobic running, 1½ to 2½ hours
Sunday	Jogging, 1 hour

For 4 weeks:

Monday	Fast relaxed running, 8 x 200 meters
Tuesday	Long aerobic running, 1 to 1½ hours
Wednesday	Time trials, 5,000 meters
Thursday	Easy fartlek running, ½ to 1 hour
Friday	Relaxed striding, 6 x 200 meters
Saturday	Long aerobic running, 1½ to 2½ hours
Sunday	Jogging, 1 hour

For 1 week:

Monday	Easy fartlek running, ½ to ¾ hour
Tuesday	Long aerobic running, 1 hour
Wednesday	Time trials, 3,000 meters
Thursday	Repeat Monday's session
Friday	Jogging, ½ hour
Saturday	Repeat Tuesday's session
Sunday	Easy fartlek running, ½ hour

For 1 week:

Monday	Jogging, ¾ hour
Tuesday	Time trials, 2,000 meters
Wednesday	Jogging, ¾ hour
Thursday	Jogging, ½ hour
Friday	Jogging, ½ hour; or rest
Saturday	Marathon race
Sunday	Jogging, ¾ to 1 hour

Continuation: jog easily for 7 to 10 days, then:

Monday	Easy fartlek running, ¾ to 1 hour
Tuesday	Long aerobic running, 1 to 1½ hours
Wednesday	Time trials, 3,000 meters
Thursday	Repeat Tuesday's session
Friday	Jogging, 1 hour
Saturday	Time trials, 5,000 meters
Sunday	Jogging, 1½ hours or more

EXPERIENCED RUNNERS

For as long as possible:

Monday	Long aerobic running, 1 hour
Tuesday	Long aerobic running, 1½ hours
Wednesday	Easy fartlek running, 1 hour, on hills
Thursday	Repeat Tuesday's session
Friday	Jogging, 1 hour
Saturday	Long aerobic running, 2 hours or more
Sunday	Repeat Tuesday's session

For 4 weeks:

Monday	Hill springing, steep hills or step running, 1 hour
Tuesday	Long aerobic running, 1½ hours
Wednesday	Time trials, 5,000 meters
Thursday	Repeat Monday's session
Friday	Leg speed, 10 x 100 meters
Saturday	Easy fartlek running, 1 hour
Sunday	Long aerobic running, 2 hours or more

For 4 weeks:

Monday	Repetitions, 15–20 x 200 meters
Tuesday	Long aerobic running, 1½ hours
Wednesday	Time trials, 5,000 meters
Thursday	Easy fartlek running, 1 hour
Friday	Leg speed, 10 x 100 meters
Saturday	Time trials, 10,000 meters
Sunday	Long aerobic running, 2 hours or more

For 2 weeks:

Monday	10–12 x 100-meter wind sprints (one every 200 meters)
Tuesday	Long aerobic running, 1½ hours
Wednesday	Time trials, 5,000 meters
Thursday	Repeat Tuesday's session
Friday	Easy fartlek running, ½ hour
Saturday	Time trials, 25 kilometers
Sunday	Jogging, 1½ hours

For 1 week:

Monday	10–12 100-meter wind sprints (one every 200 meters)
Tuesday	Long aerobic running, 1½ hours
Wednesday	Time trials, 3,000 meters
Thursday	Easy fartlek running, 1 hour
Friday	Jogging, ½ hour
Saturday	Time trials, 20 kilometers
Sunday	Jogging, 1½ hours

For 1 week:

Monday	20 x 45-meter wind sprints (one every 100 meters)
Tuesday	Easy fartlek running, ¾ hour
Wednesday	Jogging, 1 hour
Thursday	Repeat Wednesday's session
Friday	Jogging, ½ hour
Saturday	Time trials, full marathon
Sunday	Repeat Wednesday's session

For 1 week:

Monday	Jogging, 1 hour
Tuesday	Repeat Monday's session
Wednesday	Time trials, 5,000 meters
Thursday	Jogging, 1½ hours
Friday	Jogging, 1 hour
Saturday	Repeat Wednesday's session
Sunday	Long aerobic running, 2 hours

For 1 week:

Monday	10 x 100-meter wind sprints (one every 200 meters)
Tuesday	Long aerobic running, 1½ hours
Wednesday	Time trials, 3,000 meters
Thursday	Easy fartlek running, 1 hour
Friday	Jogging, ½ hour
Saturday	Time trials, 10,000 meters
Sunday	Jogging, 1½ hours

For 1 week:

Monday	20 x 45-meter wind sprints (one every 100 meters)
Tuesday	Easy fartlek running, 1 hour
Wednesday	Time trials, 3,000 meters
Thursday	Jogging, 1 hour
Friday	Jogging, ½ hour
Saturday	Time trials, 5,000 meters
Sunday	Jogging, 1½ hours

For 1 week:

Monday	Easy fartlek running, ¾ hour
Tuesday	Time trials, 2,000 meters
Wednesday	Jogging, 1 hour
Thursday	Jogging, ½ hour
Friday	Jogging, ½ hour; or rest
Saturday	Marathon race
Sunday	Jogging, 1 hour

Continuation (recovery):

Monday	Jogging, 1 hour
Tuesday	Jogging, 1½ hours
Wednesday	Repeat Monday's session
Thursday	Easy fartlek running, 1 hour
Friday	Jogging, ½ hour
Saturday	Repeat Monday's session
Sunday	Repeat Tuesday's session

Continuation (race track):

Monday	10 x 100-meter wind sprints (one every 200 meters)
Tuesday	Long aerobic running, 1½ hours
Wednesday	Time trials, 3,000 meters
Thursday	Easy fartlek running, 1 hour
Friday	Jogging, ½ hour
Saturday	Race, 5 or 10 kilometers
Sunday	Long aerobic running, 1½ hours or more

Bibliography

Anderson, Bob, and Henderson, Joe, eds. *Guide to Distance Running.* Mountain View, Calif.: World Publications, 1971.

Andrew, G. M., Guzman, C. A., and Becklake, M. R. "Effect of Athletic Training on Exercise Cardiac Output." *Journal of Applied Physiology,* no. 21 (1966).

Balke, Bruno. "Effects of Altitude on Maximum Performances." *Track & Field News.* Track technique, no. 18. Los Altos, Calif., 1964.

Bowerman, William J. *Coaching Track and Field.* Boston: Houghton Mifflin Co., 1974.

Costes, Nick. *Interval Training.* Mountain View, Calif.: World Publications, 1972.

Haggard, H. W., and Greenberg, L. A. *Diet and Physical Efficiency.* New Haven: Yale University Press, 1933.

Merton, P. A. "Problems of Muscular Fatigue." *British Medical Bulletin,* no. 12 (1956).

Morehouse, Laurence, and Miller, Augustus T. *The Physiology of Exercise.* St. Louis: The C. V. Mosby Co., 1967.

Morehouse, L. E., and Rasch, P. J. *Sports Medicine For Trainers.* Philadelphia: W. B. Saunders Co., 1963.

Potts, Frank C. "Running at High Altitude." *Track & Field Quarterly,* January 1968.

Runner's World, eds. *The Complete Diet Guide: For Runners and Other Athletes.* Mountain View, Calif.: World Publications, 1978.

Runner's World, eds. *The Complete Runner.* Mountain View, Calif.: World Publications, 1974.

Runner's World, eds. *Runner's Training Guide.* Mountain View, Calif.: World Publications, 1973.

Runner's World, eds. *Running with Style.* Mountain View, Calif.: World Publications, 1975.

Sterner, John. "Stroke and Heat Exhaustion in Athletes." *Track & Field News.* Track Technique, no. 25. Los Altos, Calif., 1966.

Van Aaken, Ernst. "Running and the Chemistry of the Blood." *Track & Field News.* Track Technique, no. 3. Los Altos, Calif., 1961.

Watts, D. C. V., and Wilson, Harry. *Middle and Long Distance, Marathon and Steeplechase.* London: British Amateur Athletic Board, undated.

Zierler, K. L. *Mechanism of Muscle Contraction and its Energetics.* St. Louis: The C. V. Mosby Co., 1961.

Index